Ocracoke Odyssey

A Naturalist's Reflections
on Her Home by the Sea

Pat Garber

With Illustrations and Photographs by the Author

Down Home Press, Asheboro, NC

ISBN 1-878086-70-7

Library of Congress Catalog Card Number

99-072696

Printed in the United States of America

Cover art by Pat Garber

Cover design by Tim Rickard

Book design by Beth Hennington

Down Home Press

P.O. Box 4126

Asheboro, N.C. 27204

*In celebration of
all the wild things
at Ocracoke*

Acknowledgements

Thanks once again to the people at the *Island Breeze*, where these stories first appeared in different form; to friends and family at Ocracoke and elsewhere, whose love and support have sustained and enriched me; to my parents, Don and Mary Garber, who continue to encourage me in whatever I undertake; and to my father's sister, Aunt Betty, whose generous gift to me upon her death made possible the purchase of my home, Marsh Haven, where much of this book takes place.

Table of Contents

Introduction

Ocracoke Island is one of the barrier islands of North Carolina. Seventeen miles long and accessible only by ferry, it is part of the Cape Hatteras National Seashore. Nestled at its southwest tip is a 750-acre fishing village where approximately 700 people reside. I fell in love with Ocracoke on my first visit in 1985, and, with the exception of a five-year stint in Arizona, I have lived on the island ever since. Island life has not always been easy, but it has always been exciting and fulfilling.

After completing my first book, *Ocracoke Wild*, which appeared in 1995, I changed my status on the island from that of transient, or "drifter" as one reviewer called me, to that of homeowner. It was a change that subtly but profoundly affected my life. After years of hoping and wishing, I was enabled by fate and the largess of my father's sister Aunt Betty (who left me enough money upon her death for a substantial down payment) to purchase the little house in the marsh where I had lived when I first moved to Ocracoke. During the 10 years I was away it had been enlarged and remodeled, so that while it was still small and simple, it was no longer primitive.

As a result of my purchase, I found that I was no longer an outsider writing about things that I loved, but to which I felt no permanent connection. They were now extremely personal. That transfer of papers, those signatures on the dotted lines (along, of course, with the transfer of a large amount of cash) made me not only the owner but also the protector of a small but ecologically rich piece of Ocracoke. Living here with my old feline friends Squirt and Scamper, I found that I no longer had to traverse the island to discover the wonders of nature; abundant and fascinating miracles were taking place right at my doorstep. Mother Nature displayed all her rampant beauty for me as I sat in my porch swing or gazed out my bedroom window. I had only to keep my ears and eyes open and in tune.

My house is a small, cedar-shake, two-bedroom cottage, an eclectic combination of rustic and Victorian architecture, located at the end of a narrow road. It has been described as a gingerbread house, a storybook cottage, a doll house. It is surrounded on three sides by salt marsh and woods and is so enveloped by the branches of wax myrtle, cedar, and yaupon trees that it is barely visible. A canal, or "ditch" as it called on the island (I prefer to call it a creek,) 12 feet wide and maybe four feet deep, comes to within a few yards of the

front door. In the distance, approximately two football fields away, is the shore of Pamlico Sound, that vast estuarine body which borders Ocracoke Island and reaches to the mainland, both separating it from and connecting it to the real world over there.

Marsh Haven, as I have named my home, is hardly recognizable as the tiny, primitive place in which I resided 14 years ago, wrapping up in blankets to stay warm and accessible only with a four-wheel-drive for much of the year. A second story bedroom with a balcony and a crystal chandelier has been added. The kitchen is now a separate (though still tiny) room, and the bath contains a luxurious old clawfoot tub, hand-laid tile, and an antique brass candle sconce. The kerosene heater has been replaced by a radiator and a propane gas fireplace with a finely molded mantle. There is even a combination washer/dryer, a television, and a word processor on which I write.

In spite of the changes, the allure of the place remains the same. The crash of the ocean surf, gentled by distance into a melodic and constant murmur, still forms the background music, and the marsh grasses still rustle in answer to the stirring of the wind. From the window by my bed I can watch pelicans and ospreys as they glide over the sound, marsh hawks as they hunt in the marsh, and fish crows as they bicker and converse in the branches of a live oak tree. From the swing on my wrap-around porch I can listen to otters as they splash and squeal in the creek, cicadas as they drone away lazy summer afternoons, and chuck-will's-widows and tree frogs as they welcome summer evenings.

Attaining the security of my own home brought me unspeakable joy, but it did it not mean that life became easier. A mortgage payment of considerable size now hovered over me, and I still did not have a "real" full-time job. I did everything from writing to cottage cleaning, from painting wildlife scenes to painting a motel. I found myself unable to renege on the responsibilities I had taken on working with homeless cats and injured wildlife, so much of my work was unpaid. Simplicity was the creed I tried to live by. I learned not to worry and I always managed to get by.

Being a woman alone on an island has provided its own special joys and sorrows. My dog, cats, and the injured birds that come and go are my family. My neighbors are the otters and herons, the turtles and tree frogs that live around me. I have friends that I can call on, and there was a special partner, gone now, who came and stayed for a while. But loneliness has been a constant  specter, haunting my nights and casting a shadow over my days. There is no one to help with that unexpected bill or to assist in climbing under the house to wrap pipes when cold weather sets in. There is no one with whom to stand in awe beneath a moonlit sky; or to share the heartbreak of having a warbler die in one's hand. Yet being alone has made me strong, and that strength allows me to follow a path of my own choosing. It is this path, my personal odyssey among the wild things of Ocracoke Island, that I write about in these pages.

My shining palace

The progression of our lives is measured, I think, not in increments of time—minutes, hours, or days—but in moments of emotional poignancy, which become encapsulated in our subconscious minds and emerge as memories. These moments, good or bad, determine how and where we go in our lives; our memories of them determine how we perceive ourselves, and in the end, who we are. It was such a moment that I experienced in the winter of 1994, sitting one evening on the porch of a small cottage surrounded by salt marsh and maritime forest on Ocracoke Island.

I had lived in this house 10 years before, spending a year of pain and joy which etched itself permanently on my psyche. I had not returned, even though I had resided within two miles of it for the past three years. I wanted desperately to make it my home; but knowing that I did not have the financial capabilities to buy it I avoided the emotions I knew it would evoke by avoiding the cottage itself.

Calvin Wilkerson had moved it to this spot 20 years before and had gradually remodeled what had been a two-room shack into a home of indescribable charm and quaintness. He knew how much I loved it. He invited me to come see it whenever I ran into him, teasing me with offers to sell it to me. But I was sure that prospect was hopeless.

Now, however, I had received an unexpected sum of money; and I was in a position, if not to buy the house, at least to allow myself to dream. And so on this dark moonless night, feeling anchorless and terribly alone, I rode my bicycle back down the road and sat again on the porch where I had spent so many hours 10 years earlier.

Memories flooded back. A westerly breeze stirred the cedar branches and the Atlantic Ocean murmured softly in the distance. They seemed to be whispering to me, "Come home." I knew then how much I wanted to be here again. I suddenly had a purpose in life; a goal. I determined on that night that if there were any way possible, I would make the little cottage in the marsh my home again.

When I was a skinny, tow-headed child growing up in Short Pump, Virginia, my mother used to recite her favorite poems to me. I can remember sitting beside her as she ironed my father's shirts or pulled the strings out of green beans grown in her garden, repeating the rhythmic lines of poets who had immortalized their dreams in words. These short stanzas by Edna St. Vincent Millay must have been among her favorites, for they were oft-repeated, and they made a lasting impression on me.

Over on the solid rock the ugly houses stand
Come and see my shining palace built upon the sand.

I knew their origin from a lesson taught at a Baptist Bible School I attended one summer with a childhood friend. It was a parable, told by Jesus and recorded in the Gospel Luke, espousing the wisdom of building one's house upon a safe and solid foundation of rock, where the floods can not wash it away, and living one's life accordingly. Edna St. Vincent Millay rejects this advice in her poem and chooses the other path, snubbing her nose at the conventional wisdom.

My mother had, unbeknownst to her, instilled in me a desire to follow that other path; to frolic with danger and tempt fate. Not for me the safety and security of the solid rock; no ugly house for this woman-child. I was constantly treading in quicksand, racing along shifting shores, searching for that shining palace.

After many wanderings and the anguished death of an ill-fated marriage, I moved to Ocracoke Island in 1984. I spent a year in a tiny two-room cottage overlooking Pamlico Sound, and while there, the words of Edna St. Vincent Millay's poem returned to echo through my mind. My tiny house, unheated and cut off from the world, at the end of an often impassable sandy lane surrounded by salt marsh, might not have been some peoples' idea of a shining palace. To me it was, as was the island of Ocracoke itself.

The hurricanes and nor'easters that tore around it in unmitigated fury, forcing the marsh grasses to bow to the ground, lashing the house with wildly thrashing cedar branches, and beckoning the water of the sound to rise and take back its own, enhanced the vision conjured by Millay's poem. The financial insecurity which accompanied my lifestyle furthered that impression as well. No nine-to-five job here, with paid vacations, health insurance, and a retirement plan in 20 years. Making ends meet at Ocracoke meant living by my wits. In that first year I cleaned motel rooms, stuffed insulation in houses, cooked and waitressed, helped put the ceiling up in the Coast Guard Station, pulled the heads off of shrimp, pedaled ice cream cones, and sold a few photographs and paintings. I did manage to make ends meet, but barely. To keep down the cost of living I caught my own fish and crabs, grew my own vegetables, and wrapped up in blankets and cats to stay warm. But I was living in my shining palace, and I envied no one.

Ten years later, after assorted adventures and numerous temporary residences, I returned to the little house in the marsh, now renovated, this time engaging in business deals with the owner and a bank to purchase it. The transaction took place despite the seemingly impossible obstacles mounted by my lack of job security or any substantial income. (The first loan officer I approached laughed out loud when I told him my financial circumstances.) It took place in spite of the fact that another potential buyer had already signed a contract on it and had obtained financing. (His car caught fire the first time he headed down to Ocracoke with the papers, burning them up, and Hurricane Gordon conveniently made landfall here the day before his second appointment. He decided that he was being given a message and changed his mind.)

So I can now claim my own little piece of Ocracoke, and I am the queen of my very own shining palace. But what does it mean to "own" a piece of land that is a constantly moving, perpetually changing, always at the mercy of the wind and the waters that surround it? What exactly is this barrier island we call Ocracoke?

Until recently, many scientists believed that the Outer Bank islands were overlays of sand riveted to a series of Pleistocene coral reefs that ran alongside the coastline. An exploratory drilling expedition in the sixties, however, found no solid base beneath the Banks. Instead it found layers of sand, about 30 feet thick, sitting upon another, older layer of sand. In truth, they were not fixed islands at all, but dynamic geological systems in a constant state of change.

Today most geologists believe that Ocracoke, along with North Carolina's other barrier islands, began to take shape about 18,000 years ago, when glaciers in Greenland and Antarctica started to melt. The water level in the ocean rose approximately 400 feet, and the coastline retreated accordingly. As the ocean gradually covered what had been solid land, a ridge of beach dunes, 40 miles east of where the Outer Banks stand today, remained above sea level, forming a string of barrier islands. As sea level continued to rise over the next 13,000 years, the islands were forced westward, toward the mainland. About 5,000 years ago the rise of sea level slowed to about one foot per century, and since then the islands have slowly migrated to their present positions. Sea level is still rising today, and the Outer Banks are still migrating inland, moving up the gentle slope of the coastal plain at about 100 to 1,000 feet for every one-foot rise in sea level.

How does this movement take place without destroying the integrity of the islands? Barrier islands participate in what scientists describe as a "sand-sharing" system. The sand on the Outer Banks is constantly moving, being washed out to sea by heavy waves; blown or carried longshore, or sideways, by currents in what is called "littoral drift"; or pushed across the islands as "overwash." When overwash occurs in big storms, sand is removed from the ocean side and deposited on the inland side. The marshes are pushed farther into the sounds, and the entire island gradually moves inland. It is this sand-sharing ability that allows the islands to continue to exist, instead of being inundated by the rising seas. This process, however, so necessary to the long-term health of the Outer Banks, has no respect for individual beaches, homes, or properties. Their existence always lies at the mercy of the elements.

Ocracoke, scientists believe, is actually made up of two islands; an older more stable one which forms the basis for the village, and a younger strip of sand, most of which is now part of the Hatteras National Seashore, which is moving faster and has wrapped itself around the earlier one.

Ocracoke, however, is composed not only of sand. It is made of marshes and maritime forests, ancient peat bogs and modern hotels and shops. It is made of fragments of other lives, bits of shell and bone from mollusks and pelicans and whales who lived and died here thousands of years ago; weathered timbers from ships lost off her shores; barely visible pilings marking long-ago goals and aspirations. It is made of people whose ancestors have lived here for hundreds of years, clinging stubbornly to a way of life that was hard and often dangerous. It is made of newcomers who have abandoned the security of more conventional lives elsewhere to follow their dreams, to find their own shining palaces. It is made of visitors who are still dreaming.

Ocracoke is an island of memories; of dreams; of poems, some of which have made their way to paper, others that exist only in the subconscious of the island psyche. Today, as I write, a westerly gale is blowing around me, causing the eaves to whistle and the cedar branches to beat out an erratic rhythm against my windows. The tourmaline waters have spilled out of the creek beside my house and I

can see them rising in my yard, cutting a channel along my flower bed where no waterway was planned. It reminds me of the temerity of my decision to live my life as I do; and that I may one day pay the price for abandoning the safety of the rock, choosing instead the beauty and capriciousness of a "shining palace built upon the sand."

Some of my favorite neighbors: diamondback terrapins

"Marsh Haven," as its name implies, is nestled against the edge of a salt marsh; a burnished plain of spartina grass and needlerush. On the other side lies Pamlico Sound, accessible by several small roads that lead to it. It is an easy matter to stroll to the sandy beach from my house or to launch my kayak at the end of one of those roads.

Hidden behind that vast curtain of marsh grass, which runs beside Pamlico Sound the length of the island, is a labyrinth of secret corridors. Winding creeks, invisible only a few feet away, suddenly open up when you paddle close and invite you to enter a wonderful hidden world—the inmost reaches of the salt marsh. The salt water creeks are home to blue crabs, mussels, young fish, shrimp, and diamondback terrapins. Paddling my kayak quietly through the marsh creeks is, for me, a kind of therapy. I love to go there anytime, but especially when I am feeling blue. They provide spiritual sustenance and bring peace when my spirit is troubled. I also enjoy sharing their magic with others. Taking small groups of tourists on kayak tours along the sound was one of the many ways in which I earned my living when I moved to Marsh Haven.

"There goes one," I exclaimed, pointing toward my right. "Over there too," moving my hand quickly toward a spot nearby. But by the time my companions shifted their gaze, there was nothing to see. The water in the creek ahead of us was a smooth steel gray, with barely a ripple breaking its polished surface.

I and several other kayakers had embarked at the edge of a small "ditch" leading into the wider embrace of the creek, and were now paddling out toward Pamlico Sound. I was leading the group on a tour of the creeks and marshes that bordered the western edge of Ocracoke Island. It was spring, and the chill waters around us were gradually warming up. We had examined fiddler crabs as we launched our little vessels, and had spotted a tri-colored heron and several great egrets as we paddled out. I had just suggested that they keep a look out for the little heads that might pop up above the surface, when several appeared. They were quick, however, and as soon as they saw us they retreated. It took several minutes before everyone was able to pick out the swift movements of the triangular heads that peered up like periscopes to look at us and then quietly disappear below the water's surface.

They belonged to some of my favorite Ocracoke neighbors, the diamondback terrapins. The creeks and sound here are home to count-less numbers of these medium-size turtles, but they usually stay out of sight. Sometimes as I paddle along I can make out the shadow of one passing below my kayak; and on certain days during mating sea-son they forget to be shy and I can watch them playing follow-the-leader, the smaller male always tagging behind the fe-male. But usually I just see the little heads, appearing briefly and gone again before I can finish a sentence.

Diamondback terrapins, (*Malaclemys terrapin*) are the smaller cousins of the well-known giant sea turtles which clamber up on

Ocracoke's ocean shoreline each summer to lay their eggs. They used to be quite common throughout the salt and brackish creeks and bays of the Atlantic coast. Today, as a result of habitat destruction and overfishing, they are much rarer, so it is nice to see so many of them here at Ocracoke. They are vigorous, fast-swimming turtles, up to eight inches in length, with sculptured carapaces (or shells,) small pale spotted heads, and large black eyes. There are seven subspecies, ranging from Cape Cod to Texas. Pamlico Sound is home to the Northern and Carolina subspecies.

Diamondbacks are the only members of the Emydid family, (a broad group of turtles with large webbed back feet for swimming) which can live in brackish or salt water. They are able to do this by means of orbital salt glands which excrete excess sodium, or salt, ions from their bodies, thus maintaining osmotic balance. The salt is expelled in "tears" through the eyes.

Like other reptiles, these terrapins are cold-blooded, and become dormant when temperatures drop. They spend the winter buried in the mud, but dig out when spring comes, or even on exceptionally warm days in winter, to swim in the creeks and sounds. There they forage for a variety of mollusks, crustaceans, worms, and other invertebrates, particularly fiddler crabs, which live on the edge of the marsh, and periwinkles, the little snails which climb up and down the stems of marsh cordgrass. They are also scavengers, and consume some plant matter.

They mate in the water, at night or early in morning, in early spring. Later, sometime between April and July, the female climbs out of the water during a daytime high tide, digs triangular or flask-shaped nests four to eight inches deep, and lays four to 18 oblong, pinkish-white, leathery eggs. She may repeat this several times in one season.

The eggs hatch in the fall, and soon the hatchlings bury in the mud to hibernate. Late arrivals may winter over in the nest. They grow approximately one inch per year for the first several years, and as they grow the scutes on the shell are pushed up into the diamond-shaped carapace that gives them their name. Males, which are smaller than females and have longer, wider tails, normally reach breeding age at three years, females not until their sixth year. If undisturbed they can live 40 years or more.

In some areas of coastal Florida terrapins are considered bad luck, according to Jack Rudloe, author of *Time of the Turtle*. They are known as wind turtles, because according to local superstition they bring the storm winds. On the other hand, Dr. David Phelps, archaeologist at East Carolina University, says that native North Carolina Indian groups may have held them sacred. Diamondback terrapin shells were found in a Tuscarora burial site on the Roanoke River, across the sound. They were part of the shaman's medicine kit, probably considered sacred objects.

The little turtles have few enemies besides humans, but sometime around the turn of the century we humans managed, in response to a fad that swept through the wealthier elements of our society, to bring them to the point of extinction. The fad was Terrapin Stew.

Native Americans and other coastal people had been eating diamondback terrapins for centuries without any serious impact on their populations, but around 1900 terrapins became big business. They were harvested up and down the coast, the northern species being considered the most desirable, and served at the most elite restaurants. Beaufort, North Carolina, had a particularly big operation. At the peak of their popularity terrapins brought 90 dollars per dozen and, says naturalist Archie Carr, were "surrounded by an aura of superlative elegance as synthetic as the latest Paris fashion."

Here at Ocracoke some of the local fishermen participated in the business. "I've caught a lot of diamondback terrapins," remembers Clinton Gaskill, now 90 years old. "We'd take a stick and run it up under a creek bank. They'd stick their heads out and we'd run and catch them. Then we'd put them in barrels and feed them fish or crab till a man would come down from Baltimore and buy them." Other fishermen fenced off small areas of the creeks to hold the live terrapins while waiting for a buyer.

Fortunately for the little reptiles, the fad died out; partly, no doubt, because of the scarcity and rising prices, but also as a result of Prohibition, since wine was an important ingredient of the recipe. Today there is still limited harvesting of diamondback terrapins, mostly as bycatch in other fisheries. I've tasted terrapin, but I can't say I was wild about it (perhaps because I kept picturing those little turtle heads peering up at me with their periscopic eyes)!

Diamondbacks have been making a gradual comeback in recent years, but the draining and development of coastal wetlands prevent their re-establishment in many of their original habitats. Pollution and siltation from human activities also have a negative effect in certain areas. Even crabpots can provide a hazard for them in fishing areas, such as Ocracoke, for they sometimes swim into them seeking the crab bait and will drown if they are trapped underwater for too long. Whenever I paddle along the shoreline of Pamlico Sound I check derelict crabpots, torn loose by past storms, in search of terrapins to rescue.

Mostly, I enjoy watching for their heads to pop up here and there in the creeks when I go kayaking. I can't help but wonder what they think as they peer up from their watery home to gaze at the strange human creatures gliding along beside them. It must seem a bit like our whale-watching excursions!

Bonnie and Clyde of
the animal world: the minks

Cape Hatteras National Seashore was established in 1953, encompassing all of Ocracoke Island except for the 775 acres that comprise the village. It was unpopular at first with many native Ocrakokers, because it required requisitioning private land. Since then, however, it has proven to be a godsend for the island itself, protecting it from the rampant development that has ravaged many Atlantic beaches.

When I moved back to Ocracoke in 1991, I became a V.I.P. (Volunteer in the Park) at the National Seashore, working with the wild ponies, the sea turtle nesting patrol, trash collection on the beach, and shorebird monitoring. My volunteering gave me the opportunity not only to assist in work I considered important, but to interact with and learn about many of nature's most intriguing actors. Since moving to Marsh Haven I have, for various reasons, had less time to volunteer; but whenever I get a chance I try to participate. As always, the rewards I receive from my experiences far exceed any amount of money that I might otherwise be paid for my time.

I stood quietly and held my breath as I peered through the scope at the distant spit of sand, watching for any sign of movement. Seeing none, I picked up my tripod and crept closer. Again I set up the scope, steadying its three spindly legs in the sand. I pulled my sweater tightly around me, chilled by this damp overcast morning, cool for early May, and by the sense of foreboding I felt. I carefully scanned the viewing area again. There was still no sign of life.

Yesterday there had been a nest there, a slight indentation in the sand where a female piping plover sat on three lightly speckled, gray-brown eggs. Nearby her mate had hovered anxiously, darting here and there and calling out in his clear piping voice, warning me not to come too close. I was participating in a National Park Service monitoring project and had been watching the pair since they had first begun to sit, about a week earlier. The pair was one of four being studied at the north end of Ocracoke, in the vast flat sandy area between the dunes and the ocean where piping plovers like to nest. They were hard to detect at first. Light tan in color with white undersides and black collars and not more than seven inches long, they blended well with their environment; but I soon learned to spot their quick motions. I enjoyed watching the plucky little birds as they tended their nests or darted along the shoreline pecking worms and small crustaceans from the wet sand. Included on the Endangered Species List, they were disappearing rapidly from Atlantic beaches, and nesting failure was one of the main reasons. The participants in the monitoring project were trying to determine what was going wrong.

I slowly moved closer, hoping I would find that I had been mistaken; perhaps watching the wrong hillock or blinded by the sunlight, and that the nest was still there. But soon there was no doubt. I now stood in the spot where the plovers had so recently guarded their nest. I saw no sign of the birds or of their eggs.

What I did see, however, were tracks—lots of them...just like at the other nest. For this was a repeat performance. The last nest of eggs I had watched had met the same unfortunate end. I studied the tracks carefully, following them as they meandered back over the dunes. They were small and closely resembled the tracks of a domestic cat. I was not, in fact, certain they did not belong to one of the feral cats that roam the island.

But participants in the study were beginning to suspect another culprit, and evidence was mounting against him. We believed that the marauder was one of the island's most ferocious predators: *Mustela vison*, known more commonly as a mink. We knew that these aquatic members of the weasel family were numerous on Ocracoke Island; I had seen one only a few days before crossing the road on its way to the dunes, perhaps in search of a piping plover nest.

Minks, along with weasels, ermines, ferrets, and polecats, are carnivores belonging to the genus *Mustela*. They live throughout the eastern United States wherever there is water and sufficient food. They measure from 18 to 28 inches in length, with males being considerably larger than females. Set low to the ground, they have long, lithe bodies with short legs, small heads, and dark coats with white spots on their throats and chins.

When frightened or agitated they produce a foul-smelling odor from which their previous scientific name, *Putorium* (Latin for rotten or smelly) derived. The Cherokee Indians of western North Carolina have a story about how the mink came to smell bad. Mink was a terrible thief, so the other animals decided to punish him by throwing him in a large fire. When he began to smell like roasted meat, they decided that he had learned his lesson, so they pulled him out. Mink, however, was unrepentant; so still a thief, he retained the odor, which he gives off when upset.

Most people are familiar with minks as components of coats and stoles, for which their soft, dark, lustrous furs have been immensely popular. Minks used to be trapped and hunted with dogs, particularly in the northern part of their range where their pelts are thickest, but today most are raised on farms. Mink trapping and farming are decreasing as the result of animal rights protests and the declining popularity of fur coats.

Although they are seldom seen, minks are still plentiful in many

areas, where they live in dens along creek beds or marshes and range far afield in their hunting. They are excellent swimmers and divers and have voracious appetites, consuming small mammals, fish, frogs, insects, bird eggs and nestlings. Normally solitary animals, males and females join together to raise their families, mating in early spring. Females are polyestrous, which means that implantation can be delayed. Although it may be longer, most litters are born in April or early May, and consist of three to six cigarette-sized young. They are weaned at about five weeks, but stay with the parents until well into the summer. They may live for 10 years.

The minks on Ocracoke had been known to attack and kill duck-lings in the village, and they sometimes put in a surprise appearance at the creek beside my house hoping, no doubt, to catch an unsus-pecting clapper rail or locate a nest of turtle eggs. I rather like the gutsy little marauders, in spite of their murderous nature. They are, after all, part of the natural world and are legitimate players in the web of life.

Or are they? There is some question as to whether minks are truly indigenous to Ocracoke Island. The National Park Service is particularly concerned about the increasing abundance of minks be-cause of the danger they pose to the piping plovers and other nesting shore birds. They have been trying for a number of years to deter-mine if the minks living on the island are native inhabitants or if they had been introduced in a fur-raising enterprise. If they are an intro-duced species, not native to the island environment, the rangers hope to trap and remove them. If, on the other hand, they are indigenous they will be allowed to stay.

Several islanders assert that minks were deliberately brought to Ocracoke in recent times. Mink sightings, however, were documented in studies from the 1930s and late '40s. It may be that minks are indigenous to the island, but that their numbers were greatly increased by the artificial introduction of a new population. The jury is still out, the verdict not yet returned. But as in other court cases, the ac-cused is presumed innocent until proven guilty; or in this case, pre-sumed indigenous until proven introduced! So those rowdy little troublemakers—the Bonnies and Clydes of the animal world—are still free to rob nests and wreak havoc. And concerned though I am about the piping plovers, I rather hope they stay that way.

Three leaves, beware! Poison ivy

I had been living in my home for just two months when the time came for me to move out. Before buying Marsh Haven I had decided that the only way I could make my rather hefty mortgage payments and maintain the relative freedom that I enjoyed was by renting it on a weekly basis to tourists during the summer. Now it was time for the rental season to begin. My regrets at having to leave were softened by the excitement of having my first book, Ocracoke Wild, *published. Using my parents' home in Richmond, Virginia, as a base, I spent most of the summer on what is known as a "book tour"; signings, radio shows, a television spot, and library talks.*

In the midst of all the hustle and bustle I set aside a few weeks to work on an archaeological project on Hatteras Island, just north of Ocracoke, excavating the site of an Algonkian Indian village. The site was believed to have been the main village of the Croatan Chiefdom, a Late Woodland group that occupied southern Hatteras and Ocracoke Islands for about 800 years. Known also as the Hatteras Indians, they were the people to whom the famous "Lost Colony" of late sixteenth century Englishmen are believed to have turned for help after fleeing Roanoke Island.

The project was right up my alley, since I have an undergraduate degree in Native American studies and a graduate degree in cultural anthropology. I was an unpaid volunteer again, but nonetheless I was delighted to be there. I soon realized how much I had forgotten, and how much I still had to learn.

"I won't get it, I won't get it, I won't get it! (I hope.)" I prayed that the power of positive thinking would work; that if I convinced myself loudly enough, those ugly red welts would not appear, covering my arms and legs, causing me to scratch and writhe in agony. But alas, it didn't work, and I spent the next week feeling immensely sorry for myself.

I had been thrilled when I was invited to join the group of archaeologists, graduate students, and volunteers who were preparing to excavate the Croatan Indian site near Buxton. They hoped to unearth the fascinating history recorded in the midden (garbage pile) left behind by this previous civilization. Dr. David Phelps, the coordinator, was a highly respected archaeology professor at East Carolina University, and the project we were working on promised to reveal new and important secrets. When I arrived at the site I noticed that it was covered with a carpet of bright little three-leaved plants, and that the yaupon and myrtle trees were draped with curtains of these same three-leaved vines. I recognized those leaves. In fact, I had made personal, though unwelcome, acquaintance with them on a number of former occasions.

I allowed myself a moment of regret that I was wearing shorts and a tank top instead of heavy jeans and long sleeves. But I quickly sighed in resignation, philosophizing that what would be would be. There was nothing I could do about it now, except try to convince either myself or the plant (whichever would listen) that I was NOT allergic to poison ivy!

Poison ivy, that most ubiquitous and feared member of the plant kingdom, thrives in the sandy soils of Ocracoke and Hatteras Islands. It is found throughout most of the United States as well. It and its close cousin, poison oak, cause itching, discomfort, and worse reactions in millions of Americans each year. I guess that I had patches of poison ivy rash on about 50 percent of my body, but at least my face was spared. One of my fellow archaeologists had his eyes swollen shut as a result of our day in the field.

Poison ivy (*Rhus radicans*) and poison oak (*Rhus toxicodendron*) are members of the sumac family. They are hard to tell apart, but generally poison oak is a woody shrub with leaves composed of three serrated or lobed leaflets. Poison ivy can fit this description as well, but it can also take the form of a long, sinuous vine, and its leaflets can be smooth as well as serrated and lobed. The three leaflets are the main thing to remember and avoid.

The plants are not really poisonous, but they contain an oil which is made up of a chemical—urushiol—to which more than 50 percent of the human race have an allergic reaction. This chemical is so potent that one drop can make hundreds of people miserable. Other animals (with the exception of the higher primates) have no reaction, and sometimes farmers get rid of it by letting their goats eat it.

Many Native Americans, having had thousands of years to develop a resistance, are not allergic to poison ivy and poison oak. In fact, according to Alan Esheleman, author of the book *Poison Plants*, some tribes used to make a bread by mixing the leaves with acorn meal, and others used it to cure warts, ringworm, and rattlesnake bite. The Pomo Indians used the sap, which turns a deep black when exposed to air, as a dye for their baskets. On the other hand, Peter Limburg in his book *Watch Out, Its Poison Ivy!* says that the Indians treated it with respect, and that some tribes believed it had a soul and

33

mind of its own. According to him they called it "my friend" to keep from angering it.

Captain John Smith described poison ivy in his writings of 1612. He wrote that it resembled English "Yvie", but "causeth redness, itchynge, and fi-

nally blysters." Peter Kalm in 1748 explained how it got another one of its nicknames, "markweed." According to him, boys used the sap to mark their names in their "linens." The marks would not come out, and would grow blacker with each washing. Early French-Canadians called poison ivy "bois de puce," or flea-wood, because of its itchy effects.

Over the years many folk remedies evolved, including the use of coffee, cream, gunpowder, and charcoal. Jewelweed, or wild impatiens, is a wildflower with orange blossoms which has been used to cure poison ivy for centuries. It often grows near poison ivy patches, and the juices in its stem seems to neutralize the oils. It can be found today in many over-the-counter remedies.

One folk remedy was used by Fred Willard, a Buxton resident who participated in the archaeology project. After his grandfather died from a reaction to poison ivy, his father fed his children, including Fred, poison ivy sandwiches so they would develop a resistance. According to Fred it worked, but I would not recommend this as a safe method of prevention for others!

The most effective remedy, of course, is to avoid getting it in the first place. Stay away from those triple leaflets! If you are exposed to it wash immediately with soap and water (using just water without the soap may spread it more.) It supposedly takes about 10 minutes for the oils to seep into the skin, so if you can't wash it off within that time, you may be in for a rash. Baking soda baths, calamine lotion, and rubbing alcohol are all suggestions that may provide some relief. Your doctor may prescribe cortisone shots if you have a severe case.

In spite of their notoriety with people, poison ivy and poison oak fill an important ecological niche. Certain insects eat and lay eggs on the leaves. In late summer the small yellow, five-petaled flowers develop into drupes (or clusters) of little greenish-white berries, which form an important food source for a variety of birds. The birds, in their turn, help to spread and propagate more poison ivy.

I recently read a newspaper article about a small cottage industry in North Carolina that pays pickers two dollars per pound to harvest poison ivy. They process the plants and export them to Germany, where they are made into an ointment for arthritis and muscle aches. You won't find me applying for that job!

The next time I returned to the archaeological site in Buxton I made sure that I was clothed from head to foot, regardless of the heat. I tried a new preventive method recommended to me; coating myself from head to foot in a product called Tec-nu, and showering it off as soon as I got home. I may even search out a patch of Jewelweed for extra insurance. If you see me scratching after all that, you'll know that I'll be considering another hobby than archaeology.

A visitor from fairyland: the hummingbird moth

The rental season was over. I had moved back into Marsh Haven, thrilled with the knowledge that it was mine for nine whole months. During the summer I had acquired, not exactly according to plan, a new cat and dog. Miss Kelley I discovered, along with her three kittens, under a dumpster near my parents' house in Richmond. I found homes for the kittens but no one wanted the feisty little tabby momma.

Huck (short for Huckleberry Finn) was an emaciated, bedraggled doberman pinscher whom I rescued from the dog pound, intending to find him a home. I soon learned, however, that in spite of his sweet temperament he was one of the most hard-headed and unmanageable dogs I had ever known. I was afraid that if I gave him away he would just end up back in the pound again (he had already been returned once when I adopted him).

So, accompanied by my cats Squirt and Scamp, as well as my two new family members, I packed away the rental dishes, took out personal treasures and clothes, and entrenched myself as firmly as possible into Marsh Haven. I then concentrated on getting to know every blade of grass, weed and wildflower, stone and crevice of my new home.

While most of the area surrounding my house is salt marsh and

maritime forest, there is a little high ground which provides room for a yard and garden. The former owners, Andy and Calvin Wilkerson, planted hydrangeas, herbs, and zinnias, and I began adding more flowers as soon as I moved in. It is a harsh environment for grow-ing most plants; the soil is acid from the cedar trees and the wind that blows from the sound across the marsh is stressful and drying.

Salt intrusion from extremely high tides and westerly blows can interrupt the best-laid gardening plans. Plants that are native to the area do best. Still, I take pleasure in planting new flowers, vegetables, and shrubs and seeing what survives. I try to select plants that provide food for wild-life, and I enjoy watching the birds and butterflies they attract.

"Look, a hummingbird!" My sister Betsy's voice reached me as I stood washing dishes at the kitchen sink. I peered through the screen porch to where she was standing in the garden, and sure enough, a fuzzy form zoomed from flower to flower, hovering over each bright red zinnia.

I hurried down the porch steps to where Betsy, visiting for a week from Buffalo with her friend Anne Maroney, was standing. I had never seen a hummingbird at Ocracoke, though I'd often wondered if they ever came here. As we watched, however, it became apparent that the little flying form was not a typical hummingbird. The colors were not right, and it lacked the long pointed beak of the eastern ruby-throated hummingbird. Anne's voice piped out from over my shoulder where she now stood. "It's not a hummingbird. It's a hummingbird moth."

Neither Betsy nor I had ever heard of one, but as we observed closely we became convinced that she was right. Anne explained that she had seen one only once, but that her aunt had identified it. I would have been excited had it been a hummingbird, never having seen one on Ocracoke, but this was an even more intriguing discovery. I had no idea that an insect could so closely mimic a bird, and I couldn't wait to learn more about it.

Hummingbird moths, I discovered at the library, are a species of moth belonging to the hawkmoths, of the family *Sphingidae*. The hawkmoths are fairly large moths with robust bodies and small, streamlined wings. They are powerful fliers, from whence the name hawkmoth derives. Most are nocturnal but a few, including the hummingbird moths, fly during the day. They have long, well developed tongues which they use to take sap from various flowers.

Like other moths, they belong to the suborder *Heterocera*, and are distinguished from their cousins, the butterflies, by their lack of clubbed antennae. Butterflies and moths make up the order Lepidoptera, which means "scaly wings." Their wings are covered with thousands of tiny, overlapping, often brilliantly colored scales which provide the exquisite patterns for which butterflies and moths are famous. There are at least 170,000 species, ranging from the arctic tundra to tropical rainforests.

The Lepidoptera evolved in conjunction with the flowering plants that they depend on. Fossil records indicate that moths have been around for over 100 million years, butterflies for at least 40 million years. About one tenth of all Lepidoptera are butterflies, the rest moths.

While there is one explicit qualifying factor for distinguishing butterflies and moths—the clubbed tip on the antennae—there are several generalizations that usually apply in identification. Butterflies are day-flyers, whereas most moths fly at night. Butterflies usually have brighter colors. Moths generally have feathered antennae. Also, butterflies rest with their wings held together straight over the back, whereas most moths rest with their wings out to the side. So vague is the rule for distinguishing the two, however, that, according to naturalist Dr. David Sharp, the only practical definition is that "all Lepidoptera that are not butterflies are Heterocera (moths)."

Butterflies and moths share a complex life cycle composed of four phases: the egg; the larva, or caterpillar; the pupa, and the adult. Adults mate in mid-flight, and later the female lays her eggs on the plants which will later sustain them. Most of the eating is done during the larval, or caterpillar, stage. Certain kinds of caterpillars, particularly those of some moths, cause great amounts of damage during this stage—consuming and destroying the leaves of trees and crops.

A few kinds of butterflies and moths do not eat at all during their adult stages, moving swiftly toward copulation, then death; but most live off plant fluids, which they can do without harming the hosts. They have long hollow feeding tubes, known as proboscises, which they keep coiled beneath the head when not in use. Butterflies (and also the diurnal hummingbird moths) feed mostly on flower nectar, since most flowers open up during the day. Nocturnal moths feed on the few flowers that open at night, and also on plant sap and fluids in decaying plants and animals. Butterflies and moths provide an important ecological service by transmitting pollen from flower to flower as they feed.

Several kinds of hawkmoths, in both the old and new worlds, go by the common name of hummingbird moths. *Hemaris thysbe*, or the hummingbird clearwing, lives in Canada and the eastern United States. I am convinced that this is the moth Betsy, Anne and I saw. It has a wingspan of one and a half to two and a half inches, with clear patches, which give the impression of holes, on the wings. As a caterpillar it is yellowish green with pale stripes, and feeds on hawthorn and related species. It lives for about three months in its adult stage, zipping around from flower to flower, convincing naive human observers that it is not a moth at all, but a hummingbird.

This had been an incredible year for all kinds of butterflies and moths. According to a professor at the University of Richmond, this phenomenon has been observed in Virginia as well. She said that it may be the result of the extreme dryness and heat during spring and early summer. The dryness reduced the ability of the plants to defend themselves with toxic or distasteful fluids in their leaves. The larval, or caterpillar stages of the butterflies and moths, which feed on these leaves, were able to eat well and grow fast and strong. The heat would have also enabled the caterpillars to grow quickly, pupate, and emerge as adults. The swiftness of the cycles may have even led to extra generations of butterflies and moths. Whatever the cause, the proliferation of these lovely creatures increased the pleasure of summer and fall for me, culminating in my sighting of the exquisite hummingbird moth.

It seems incredible to me that after all the years I have spent studying Mother Nature, she still hides wonderful secret treasures to spring on me at unexpected moments. Discovering the previously unknown hummingbird moth at my doorstep reminded me of the limits of my knowledge. It also brought back the often forgotten thrill of childhood discovery, and carried me back, if only briefly, to a time when the entire world was a fairyland, and every butterfly and hummingbird a fairy creature.

The writing spider

Living at Marsh Haven proved to be as joyous as I had expected. Each day brought a new surprise as I became acquainted with all my neighbors. There were the stinkpot turtles, or hicka-dees as they are known locally, that lived near the cattails. There were the yellow rails and soras that darted secretively along the edges of the creek; the American bittern that I glimpsed occasionally through the blades of spartina grass. There were a number of spiders that resided within the walls of my house, keeping out of sight for the most part but snagging mosquitos in their inconspicuous webs.

I guess I could be accused of suffering from Arachnophilia; for I have to admit that I am rather fond of spiders. Not that I like to pick them up or fondle them in any way; and I'd probably jump as high as anyone if I found one climbing up my leg. But I don't mind having one or two hanging out in the corners of my house, and I find the tiny silken curtains of web that drape gracefully across the crystal chandelier in my bedroom quite elegant. When it is time to rent my house for the summer I carefully remove all the spiders I can find and re-house them in a tree or shrub outside, apologizing and explaining that my renters might not share my feelings. I was delighted though, to read in the renters' journal that one couple had not only enjoyed the spiders in my bathroom but had named them. Kindred spirits indeed.

"Wow, Come look at this," I called to my friend Don as we gathered some items for a bicycle ride along Ocracoke's Nature Trail. It was just past dawn on what promised to be a lovely October day, and I had gone into the downstairs bedroom, used mostly as an office and an art studio, to get a canteen. I pointed to the window as he walked into the room.

There, stretched across the frame and held in place by almost invisible threads of silk, was an elaborately woven tapestry. It was shaped like a spiral and bejewelled with the gossamer diamonds of an early morning dew. Don stopped and stared, as impressed as I was. "Was that there yesterday?" he asked. I shook my head. "Not that I know of. I sure didn't notice it. But is it beautiful or what?"

We admired the work of art for a few moments before looking closer for the artist. She wasn't hard to find, tucked in a ball in the hub of the web, apparently asleep. She must have worked hard last night, and certainly deserved a rest. We left her to it.

Later that afternoon, when we returned from our ride, I looked in on my guest again. She was awake now, busy at work near the center of her creation, and we could see that she was as beautiful as it was.

She was about an inch long, black with a yellow and orange design on her back. I had seen similar spiders with webs that draped between bushes in gardens, and one, earlier that summer, that stretched across my deck. She was an Orange Argiope, sometimes known as a garden or writing spider.

Argiope belong, like all spiders, to the Arachnids, which are part of the phylum

43

Arthropoda. The Arachnids, which also include scorpions, mites, and horseshoe crabs, are distinguished from other arthropods by having two instead of three body sections, their head and thorax fused into one. Attached to this cephalothorax are four pairs of legs, a pair of palpi (which resemble small legs), and a pair of mandibles. The mandibles have claws at the end, and in each claw is a small hole through which poison is injected into the spider's prey.

At the hind end of the abdomen are three pairs of spinnerets. They contain tiny tubes through which silk thread is spun to make the webs for which spiders are so famous. Different kinds of threads are produced for different purposes and different parts of the web. Similar to the material produced by silkworms, spider threads can also be made into silk cloth, though not as fine as the better known variety. Spider silk has been used to make fishing lines and nets; optical equipment and gun sights; to stop bleeding and to lower fevers.

The greatest benefit provided to humans by spiders, however, is not through their weaving but through their eating. They trap and consume huge amounts of insects, including flies, mosquitos, roaches, and garden pests.

In spite of this, spiders are far from popular themselves. Many people dislike them, and homemakers are perpetually knocking down the webs they make in the corners of rooms. Some people are afraid of them, despite the fact that they bite only in self defense. The nursery rhyme "Little Miss Muffet," (whose heroine was actually the daughter of Thomas Muffet, a naturalist who studied spiders) is a good example of this "arachnophobia."

Spiders are not always viewed so unsympathetically, however. Mythology and literature are full of stories that cast them as heroines rather than villains. Hopi stories depict Grandmother Spider as a messenger of the Sun Spirit, and the Cherokees credit her with bringing fire into the world. Spider Woman plays an important part in Navajo tradition as a teacher of weaving and a very wise woman. In Africa the spider is seen as a symbol of patience and productivity. According to Greek mythology the first spider was Arachne, a young maiden who won a weaving contest against the goddess Minerva and, in retribution, was turned into an eight-legged, full-time weaver. E.B. White's popular children's story, *Charlotte's Web,* portrays a spider as a heroine who saves the life of her friend Wilbur, the pig, by writing about him in her web.

Argiope, the spider in my window, was an orb web spider, the kind best known for beautiful webs. She had begun her life as an egg, carried first in her mother's abdomen and later deposited in a pear-shaped sack attached to or near her mother's web. She, along with hundreds of her siblings, had hatched one spring day two to three years before, and had immediately set out on an incredible adventure. Following instinct, she had spun a strong, tensile thread and launched herself into the wind. Known as "ballooning," this had carried her wherever the wind happened to blow—in this case, right to my house. Now her traveling days were over.

In her new home, she had grown and molted, grown some more and molted again, until she reached maturity at the age of two years. No doubt, she had spun many a web before the one she currently occupied. Orb web spiders often build a new web every night or so, taking approximately a half hour to complete the task.

Earlier in the year she had probably mated, after being courted by a male one fourth her size. This male most likely wooed her by plucking and beating out a rhythm on a special mating thread that he attached to her web. In spite of the romantic-sounding nature of this

45

courtship, it was hardly a tender love affair. After mating he had to make a speedy retreat or risk becoming her next dinner.

My window was an unusual spot for this kind of spider to build a web, but it must have been a good one. Argiope stayed there, giving my cats Squirt and Scamp and us an excellent daily show of spinning and repairing her web, catching her insects, wrapping them in silk, and devouring them. She wove interesting zigzag ribbons, known as stabilimentums, into the web to strengthen it. They sometimes resembled human writing, which is where Argiope obtained her nickname, the "writing spider."

One day, a week or so after I found her, I saw a new addition in the corner of the web. It was a whitish, pear-shaped cocoon. Argiope had built it in the night, using three different kinds of thread, spending more than an hour arranging them in meticulous layers. In it, I knew, were close to a hundred tiny eggs, fertilized by male sperm which Argiope had kept stored in her abdomen until the proper time for egg-laying.

The weather grew colder as winter approached. Argiope stayed in her web, catching her dinner, perhaps watching over her egg case. Then one cold morning when I glanced at the window she was gone. Her life cycle had come to an end. Left behind, however, was the egg cocoon, tucked safely in the corner of the web.

All winter it lay there, protecting first the eggs and later the tiny spiders that remained inside after they hatched. One spring morning I noticed that the cocoon had broken open and only remnants remained. Nature's promise had been fulfilled. The tiny Argiope spiderlings, looking much like miniature versions of their parents, had cut through the egg case, spun out a long thread, and gone ballooning off into the world. By now, many of them probably had perished. One or two, however, might have found a fair wind and landed in a safe haven. They would be building their own small but perfect webs. One day, when they reached adulthood, they would repeat the cycle I had witnessed.

I couldn't help thinking about my very favorite spider, Charlotte, the heroine of *Charlotte's Web*. At the end of the story, as winter approaches, she too lays her eggs and dies. When spring comes her children, like those of the Argiope in my window, cast their lines into the wind and disperse into the world. Three, however, remain behind to live in Charlotte's barn.

Whenever I see a writing spider web in my yard now, I wonder if it belongs to one of the spiderlings born in my window, carrying on in the footsteps of my friend the Orange Argiope.

A special Christmas gift:
the chuck-will's-widow

Christmas at Ocracoke is a special time. The mad hustle and bustle of the cities, the shopping mania of the suburbs, do not exist here. The shops that are open are peaceful places where one can browse and chat with the shopkeepers. Private parties and community activities such as caroling, wreath-making, and church and school productions are the highlights of the season.

I was working this particular fall at the Community Store, which sits on the edge of Silver Lake Harbor. We took orders for Christmas trees, collards, and turkeys, sold groceries and miscellaneous items, rented videos, and turned on the gasoline and diesel tanks for boaters and commercial fishermen at the end of the dock. Marty Harris made deliveries on his bicycle to those who were unable to get out to shop. The Community Store was the place to catch up on the latest news around town. Almost everyone who came in had some bit of gossip to share. I was never so "up" on community happenings as I was that year.

As before, I continued my volunteer work as a federally and state licensed wildlife rehabilitator. Though licensed to care for all kinds of animals, most of those I tended were birds. Some I happened upon myself; others were brought to me by the National Park Service or

Coast Guard; most were referred by tourists or residents.

It was late morning, almost Christmas, and in the piney woods of Ocracoke small feet trod through the fallen leaves, strewing them about, while small hands gathered pine cones for decorations. Then the hands stopped, and blue eyes in a child's face stared at an object on the ground.

Reid Newell, four-years old, was bundled against the chill of an early cold spell, as he and his mother, Sally, stared silently at a motionless brown bird near their feet. It was reddish-brown and tan, a pretty pattern of stripes and speckles, about 10 inches long. Sally thought it was dead, so still it lay. But when she reached toward it, she was startled by an odd guttural growling. Then the bird opened its beak so wide as to dwarf the rest of its body.

I was riding my bike along Lighthouse Road, on my way home from an errand, when Sally waved me down.

"We've been looking for you," she said, her face alight with excitement. "We found a strange bird up in the woods, something like an owl. It was lying still and we weren't sure it was alive, but when we got close it kind of growled and opened its beak—it's mouth was huge—but it didn't move. Do you want to see it?" Sally and Reid had come to me before when they found birds in trouble. Leaving my bike on the side of the road, I hopped into their van. Sally dropped Reid off and drove back up the beach road to the woods.

I had doubts about whether we'd find the bird again, but Sally led me right to the spot, and there it lay, camouflaged by the leaves but not entirely hidden. I had guessed from her description, and I knew immediately upon seeing it, that it was a member of the nightjar, or goatsucker, family, which includes nighthawks, whip-poor-wills and chuck-will's-widows. These birds are related to owls, and somewhat resemble them. They are insect-eaters, and they use their huge mouths to scoop up mosquitoes and other insects as they fly. They are nocturnal, and during the day lie still in the leaves, protected by camouflage.

This one was so weak that it was easy to catch. It made its strange growling sound and opened its wide mouth again, trying perhaps to scare us away, but made no effort to escape. It did not seem to be hurt, but was thin and very cold as I cradled it against my body to warm it. Sally gave me, my bike, and the little bird a ride home, and I settled it in a dark box on a heating pad. Then I looked it up in my Peterson's bird guide. It was indeed a chuck-will's-widow (*Caprimulgus carolinensis*), the largest of

the nightjars and the one most frequently found on Ocracoke. But according to the book it was a summer resident and should be far south by this time of year. To be sure, I called up the Virginia Wildlife Center where I had done my initial training in wildlife rehabilitation. A veterinarian confirmed that the bird was far north of its winter range.

"It probably is young and got caught up in a storm and blown off course," she guessed. "But it will never survive the cold there now. You need to get it to Florida as quickly as you can."

She gave me instructions on how to feed it by pushing small balls of canned dog food down its throat, but warned me that members of the nightjar family do not usually do well in captivity, so it was important to get it south as soon as possible. She also gave me the name and address of a wildlife veterinarian in Fort Lauderdale who could help.

Getting it to Florida, however, and keeping it on a constant feeding schedule in the meantime, would not be easy. I made a number of phone calls, looking for a transporter; but it was Sally who located the bird's ticket south. Linda Scarborough was planning to leave in two days, driving to Florida with her daughters, Jenny and Cathy, for the holidays. And yes, she was willing to take the chuck-will's-widow.

Meanwhile, in its cage in my bathroom, the little bird was warming up and growing much livelier. The main thing I was concerned about was giving it adequate nourishment. It was very thin. These birds require a terrific amount of calories and protein, and without this, I knew, my patient would die or be too weak to release.

I spent a good part of the next day and a half (nights included) rolling dog food balls and trying to cajole the bird into opening its cavernous mouth so I could poke them in. At first it spit out the balls, but gradually it started swallowing them. As it gained back its strength, it became harder to catch and hold, which didn't make the job any easier.

The chuck-will's-widow gets its unusual name from its distinctive four-syllable whistle, a haunting song that punctuates summer evenings in the south, similar to, but distinguishable from, that of the whip-poor-will, its larger northern cousin. The ranges of both species converge in North Carolina, but on Ocracoke the chuck-will's-widow is more common.

Like other nightjars, these birds are nocturnal. Only their courtship ritual is performed during the day. According to observers, it is quite dramatic, with the male strutting, puffing, spreading its tail, drooping its wings, and jerking its body before the female of his fancy. Once she accepts him, the two birds spend their time perching close together before nesting.

The pair does not build a nest, but deposits two mottled eggs, cream to pinkish in color, on the leafy forest floor, usually in the same spot each year. If the nest is disturbed, the parents will move the eggs (or nestlings), carrying them in their mouths to a safer spot. The eggs hatch in late spring after approximately 20 days. The nestlings are semi-precocial, which means they are covered with down at birth and are mobile, but unable to feed themselves.

They can fly in 17 days and soon learn to feed themselves, swooping through the night air with their mouths open. Bristles lining the edges of their huge mouths help them trap flying insects, and scientists believe that small stones are eaten to help in digesting hard-shelled beetles. Examinations of stomach contents have shown that they occasionally eat small birds, such as sparrows and hummingbirds, swallowed whole, as well. They feed and grow strong until autumn, at which time they set out on a long journey south for the winter, something this bird was now about to do by unconventional means.

Linda stopped by early on the morning of her departure, hoping to catch the seven o'clock ferry to the mainland. After a quick lesson in how to hold and feed the bird, she and her daughters were on their way to Florida with it.

Though not an endangered or threatened species, chuck-will's-widows are in decline due to habitat loss. This made our bird's survival all the more important as Sally, Reid and I waited for news. It came by postcard. Linda had delivered the bird safely to the rehabilitation center in Fort Lauderdale, and it had been released, thin but healthy, the next day.

Whether it survived, we will never know. But we do know that for all of us who tried to help the chuck-will's-widow, Christmas was a little more special because of our encounter with it.

A walk on the beach

My job at the Community Store ended soon after Christmas. During January and February I concentrated on gathering and drying the leaves of yaupon, a small holly tree that grows along the Outer Banks, to make into tea. There was no market for it now, but I knew that in the spring when the shops opened I would be able to sell all I could prepare. Yaupon tea was an island tradition, used originally by the early native people who lived here, later by the English-speaking colonists; a regular staple for many until a few years ago. Tourists enjoyed buying my small bags of tea leaves as tokens of old Ocracoke, and preparing them provided me with income-producing work through the lean months of winter.

My yaupon business did not take all my time, however. I spent many hours exploring the maritime forests and marshes that bordered the sound and wandering along the ocean shore. At night or in the early morning, wrapped in a blanket and usually draped with a cat or two, I recorded what I saw and felt in my journal.

It was a brisk morning in February, with sunny skies, temperatures in the 40's, and a temperamental northeast breeze; a good day for a walk on the beach. But today I did not intend to merely take a walk. I planned to walk the entire beach, 16 miles from the North End to South Point. My tuna fish sandwiches were already made, orange juice in a thermos, water in a plastic jar, dog biscuits in a bag. I tossed everything into my day pack, along with an extra pair of shoes, gloves, and a warm hat.

"Let's go, Huck!" I called to my headstrong doberman pinscher. I took his leash off its hook, held the porch door open for him, and headed to the truck. I had thought of looking for a ride to the North End, but decided that a prospective chauffeur might think I was silly, so I drove up the island and parked my truck in the northernmost lot. I slipped the leash onto Huck's collar and my shoulders into the backpack. Then we set out along the sandy winding path that led across the dunes to the sea.

I had driven this shoreline many times before as a volunteer for the National Park Service, searching for piping plovers, loggerhead sea turtles, injured birds, and trash. At various times, in short spurts, I had probably walked every inch of it. But today I decided to forget that I had been here before and try to look at everything with new eyes.

It was low tide, and I could see miles of exposed wet sand stretching along the sea. Near the dune line, the wind had sculpted the sand into whirls and rifts, with little peaks and valleys in various colors of black and tan and rose. Looking down, I imagined that this was how the surface of the moon might look to an astronaut as he descended in his spaceship. The unworldly contours were adorned with broken bits of shell—scallop and moonsnail and whelk—interwoven into the design as artistically as if an alien baker were putting the final touches on the frosting of a giant space cake.

As Huck and I walked closer to the ocean, I saw other shells,

many still whole, more recently ripped from their homes beneath the waves. Cockle shells were plentiful here, as were the colorful forms of scallops. I spied a sand dollar lying near the water, its fragile form still perfect in spite of the battering waves. A pile of feathers farther up the beach drew my attention. Walking toward it, I found the emaciated, partially eaten carcass of a common loon, wearing the soft browns of its winter plumage for its funeral attire.

Looking farther down the beach, near the high tide mark, I saw a great hulking shape, faded turquoise in color. Puzzled, I gave a tug to Huck's leash to change our direction, and we approached it. It was partially buried in sand, but I could see that it was the remains of some large wooden structure. Not far down the beach lay a similar configuration of boards, and this time its shape was more easy to distinguish. It was the remains of a boat. I let my eyes wander farther down the beach. For as far as I could see, pieces of it lay askew, intermingled with the shells, driftwood, and other remains of once-living creatures.

I remembered that the month before a fishing boat, the 74-foot trawler *Shawna Louise*, had been caught in a fierce winter storm near here. She and her crew had been battered by strong 35- mile-per-hour winds and eight-foot seas. The captain and his mates had struggled valiantly, freezing cold and soaking wet, to bring the boat back to a safe haven; but in the end they lost. They radioed ashore for help, and a Coast Guard helicopter rescued them, forcing them to leave their boat behind as the deadly ocean, once her friend and partner, claimed her for its own.

Now all that was left were these skeletal remains; flotsam they were called. Here on this piece you could see her wooden ribs, perfectly and painstakingly shaped by some caring human hand; exposed now to the sun and the eyes of any passerby. I turned aside, feeling, oddly, that I had no right to look.

Had she wrecked a few years ago, she would not still be lying on the beach. Islanders would have salvaged the precious wood, rare and hard to obtain, for homes, boats, even for firewood. Part of my own house is built with wood from a boat that wrecked here long ago.

I tried to imagine being on the *Shawna Louise* that day; the howling winds, the monstrous waves crashing across the bow, tossing her helter-skelter as the storm tore all around her. I had been caught at sea in a frightening storm on a sailboat, and I knew the terror it could inspire.

At least the crew had been saved. It must have been a dramatic moment, filled with relief and heroism as well as sadness, when the Coast Guard rescuers pulled them from the sea. The shattered *Shawna Louise* represented the end of someone's dream; but even now, I thought to myself, a new dream would be forming.

We continued down the beach, and soon Huck drew my wandering attention to another object lying in the sand. He growled softly as we approached it, and I detected the faint putrid odor of death. It was a bottlenose dolphin, or what was left of it. Like the remains of the trawler, its life force was gone now, its struggles ended, its dreams stilled.

The beach that I was hiking was not only a beautiful vista; not just a path for migrating shorebirds and restless humans with frolicking dogs. It was a graveyard; the final resting place for dolphins and whelks, for loons and sand dollars, for wrecked boats and for ravaged dreams. Walking along it, I was reminded that we are all a part of nature, close kin to everything I saw on the beach. Each sand dollar, each dolphin, each bird, had a story of its own, no less dramatic than that of the trawler; a dream that had died, a dream that would be reborn in another form.

As I wandered among the last pieces of wreckage, I saw an intriguing piece of carved wood, smoothed and rounded into what must have once been a functional design. I picked it up and slipped it into my backpack, my own bit of salvage from the *Shawna Louise*, and a reminder of my walk.

I had meandered and pondered enough for one day. Huck and I would not make it back before nightfall if we did not hurry; surely not before the dark clouds that were forming on the horizon scooted across the sea to soak and chill us. We set a steady pace, stopping only briefly to eat our lunch, to watch live dolphins surfing in the waves, to observe working trawlers filling their nets and heading back to harbor.

I was sorely tempted, when we passed the Airport Ramp, to head across the dunes to the road, especially since a misty rain was beginning to cling to my sweatshirt. But Huck and I plowed on, me with feet that were beginning to hurt, Huck still full of energy and tugging hard at the leash. We moved past a group of strangers scouring the sand for unusual shells, past a pickup truck of locals enjoying a beach ride, past more skeletons. At South Point Road we glimpsed the remains of an ancient shipwreck, formerly covered in sand but now exposed by a recent storm. Its story was hidden in the mists of time, and one could only guess at the heart-rending drama that left it there.

We reached South Point as the rain began in earnest. I stopped for a moment, rubbing Huck's ears, and stared across the inlet toward Portsmouth Island, hidden now by the clouds. Then we turned homeward and, thoroughly soaked, began plodding back. When Conk and Mickey O'Neal offered us a ride in the back of their pickup truck, I gladly accepted. We were cold and wet, but we felt great as we rushed into our warm house. I dried Huck off with a towel, turned the heater by his dog bed to high, and hopped into a steamy shower. It had indeed been a good day for a walk.

Freddy the fin whale

The months of January and February can be hard on the barrier islands of North Carolina. They are intensely beautiful but agonizingly lonely, with heavy seas, strong gales, and cold temperatures. Winter storms and heavy fog often close the roads or prevent the ferries from running. A sense of isolation envelopes those who live here. It is a time of quiet and introspection; a time that can draw people close together, yet can hone the ache of loneliness to a bitter edge. Winter at Ocracoke lays bare our most vulnerable emotions; our longings, our joys, our sorrows. It is a season for yearning, for exulting, for crying. The heavy mists that rise off the marsh can immerse you in despair, and the constant wind can make you crazy. Each year, at some point, I swear that I will never spend another winter alone at Ocracoke; yet every winter finds me here again. For never am I so in touch with my own deepest self; never do I feel so connected to the natural world in all its cruel and splendid glory.

I didn't see his majestic, tormented body; never touched his lacerated skin; never spoke to him or heard his ragged breathing. But for three days I prayed for him, and at the end of those three days I cried quietly and mourned his passing as I would a loved one. I was not alone. All along the Outer Banks and far west on the mainland people like me followed the story of the young fin whale stranded in Oregon Inlet.

No one knows how he got there, or why. But one icy cold day in early February, when most folks were trying to stay warm indoors, two hunters steered their boats out to the duck blinds and saw the huge whale lying in the shallow waters of Pamlico Sound. They called the Coast Guard, who jumped into their boats and headed out to check.

There had been a storm the night before—a nor'easter, and the tumultuous waves, aided by an extremely high tide, must have allowed him to surf over the shoals, depositing him an incredible mile and a half inland. He was lying, when they found him, in a shallow trough of waist-deep water. He bore the signs of a struggle—lacerations and small cuts, possibly from ice, but he was definitely alive and conscious.

It did not take long for word to spread. Oregon Inlet lies close to Nags Head. The locals there soon heard, and before long the news had traveled far afield that a whale was beached. He was christened with the name of "Freddy."

Rhett White, of the North Carolina Aquarium at Manteo, was contacted; and Frank Hudgins flew over Freddy and examined him from his plane. He was 44 feet long and weighed approximately 60 tons; a juvenile male, probably three to five years old. He was a fin whale, also known as a finback or razorback, because of a distinctive ridge along the back. Fin whales are among our largest cetaceans, second only to blue whales. They, like the blues, are baleen whales, belonging to the sub-order *Mysticetti* or "mustached whales." Their scientific name, *Balaenoptera physalus*, comes from the Greek word for rorqual, which means "a kind of toad that puffs itself up;" hardly a fitting name for such a regal beast.

Adult fin whales may live for up to 70 years and may reach 80 feet in length. They are found throughout the great oceans of the world. Each year they undertake long migrations from the frigid waters of the Arctic or Antarctica where they feed in summer, to the warm waters of temperate and tropical seas in winter to mate and reproduce. They usually stay far offshore, traveling in small pods of five to 10 members, sometimes congregating in large groups of 100 or more.

In spite of their huge size, they live on tiny animals that they engulf in their huge mouths along with gallons and gallons of water. Shrimp-like krill and small fish, which are strained through specialized plates in the mouth called baleen, or whalebone, make up most of their diet.

Fin whales are among the fastest of the large whales, reaching speeds of 32 kilometers per hour. They can be quite acrobatic, diving to depths of 230 meters and breaching, or leaping from the water, with great splashes. They have tall, impressive "blows," up to six meters high, which is the way they are usually spotted.

According to Farley Mowat, author of *A Whale For the Killing*, fin whales are among the most intelligent of the cetaceans. They are known in history as the friends of humans, and there is an old Scandinavian story of one defending a ship from other "bad" whales for a whole day. Their friendliness did not protect them, though, from slaughter by whalers, who sought their blubber for oil and their baleen for ladies' corsets. By the mid-twentieth century their populations were decimated. Today they are protected as part of a moratorium imposed by the International Whaling Commission in 1986, but they are still endangered by pollution, pirate whalers, and a possible weakening of the moratorium.

Freddy was just a baby. He had most likely been weaned from his mother a couple years before, and should have been far out at sea, traveling with a small group of fin whales. Somehow, though, he found himself alone, near a shoreline that was foreign to him. There is no way to know for sure if he beached himself on purpose or was too weak to resist the force of the storm as it drove him westward. The experts seem to be fairly sure, however, that something was wrong with Freddy.

His struggle to survive was valiant. Until the end he kept trying to reach deep water, but water deep enough to support his bulk was too far away. Marine biologists, engineers, National Coast Guard personnel, and people from all over the country tried to find a way to help Freddy back to the ocean, but no one could find an answer. Freddy had taken the wrong turn and sealed his fate on that cold February day. He died on February 8th, three days after he beached himself.

The necropsy was not conclusive but indicated that Freddy suffered from a heavy infestation of parasites that affected his kidneys. It may be that he knew he was ill and came ashore to die. Even so, he fought to live, and he did so for three heart-breaking days, cheered on by thousands. His passing was mourned by many.

What is it about a whale that so touches the hearts of us humans? They are certainly not fuzzy or cute, or beautiful by our usual standards. Their large size draws our attention, of course, and we may be fascinated by their unique place in the ecosystem as mammals who have rejected their home on land. We surely respect their high intelligence and complex communication system; and we may feel saddened and guilt-ridden by their swift journey toward extinction.

But there is something more—a bond of kinship that seems to

draw together humans and whales, along with their cousins the dolphins. History records countless stories about cetaceans who befriended and rescued humans, just as humans tried, this time, to help Freddy.

I can't help wondering when summer arrives and the Atlantic fin whales congregate in the far north to feed, will they be looking for the youngster we knew as Freddy? When he does not appear, will his mother, friends, or relatives worry and wonder what became of him? I wish I could let them know that he did not die unloved and unmourned; and that his passing was not purposeless, for it reawakened for many, in a very personal way, an awareness of the plight of the world's great whales.

Snapping turtles: courtship in the creek

The seasons creep up quietly at Ocracoke. Most island trees— the cedars, yaupon, wax myrtles, and live oaks—keep their garbs of greenery year-round. There is no riotous panorama of red and gold in the fall, no bursting forth of pink and white blossoms in the spring. The seasons change in little ways. One suddenly notices that the king- fisher, who has perched daily on the dead tree by the creek all winter, is not there. The horizon over the sound, sprinkled each winter morn- ing with long streams of low-flying cormorants, is suddenly empty. So, too, are the red cedars, which only a few weeks ago seemed alive with the busy antics of myrtle warblers. One day there is a flash of orange near the dune line at the beach, soon identified as the black and white, orange-beaked shape of an oyster catcher. A few days later there are two of them.

The broomstraw rush, which has curtained the creek all winter in shades of soft blush wine, is lying low against the damp ground, and beneath it one can see fresh green shoots pushing up past the dry stalks. The pewter, ash, and copper tones of the winter salt marsh turn imperceptibly but undeniably brighter, greener. One morning the joyous, lilting melody of a mockingbird, anxious to begin setting up house, resounds from the live oak cross the road. The drone of a boat motor hums from the channel as a fishermen heads out to set his gill nets. Spring has come to Ocracoke.

I was on my second cup of coffee, absently stroking my cat Squirt and finishing a quick perusal of the May 16th morning paper, when I heard a knock on the door. It was Calvin, my neighbor. "Come take a look at what's happening in the creek," he invited me. "I've never seen anything like it."

The splashing disturbed the entire creek. As we drew near, I saw what appeared to be some huge reptilian creature, perhaps an alligator. Then the creature split into two parts, each with a log-like, triangular head, an armored body, and a long, snake-like tail. The splashing stopped for a moment, and I was able to see clearly. Two huge snapping turtles, each nearly three feet long, floated on the water's surface, facing each other, circling slowly.

Are they fighting, we wondered, or are they enthralled in the raptures of love? We watched as one of the snappers, slightly larger than the other, slid forward and, moving under the water, engaged the second in a slow somersault. Round and round they circled, each occasionally lifting its head to suck in air with a raw hissing gasp.

"They're not snapping at each other," I said. "They don't seem to be mad." He agreed. We decided that they were not engaged in battle, but in that age-old springtime rite, when "a young (or old) turtle's fancy turns to love."

Calvin left to go to work, but I got my camera and came back to watch. The turtles separated for a few minutes and dove beneath the murky waters, but as I turned away, thinking the display was over, I saw them re-surface 20 feet up the creek and begin again. The activities continued all day. Calvin's cat Tiger Lily found a ringside seat on the shore and watched with fascination. I warned her not to get too close, lest she become a snapper snack. Huck barked furiously from the yard each time the turtles grew exceptionally rowdy. I slipped out every few hours to check on the turtles and snap some more photographs.

Their love-making was acrobatic but never rough. It was patient, even tender; hardly what I would have expected from ornery snapping turtles. The next day they had retreated back into the water's murky darkness, leaving no trace behind.

I already knew that snapping turtles lived here. Calvin had told me how they wreaked havoc on Tom Leonard's ducks and geese when he lived at my house and raised waterfowl. The year before, I had observed one lumbering through the yard, heading from the marsh back to its watery home, and my niece Vicki Miller had seen one crossing the road recently. But normally they kept out of sight. I had never seen one in the creek before, and certainly none that put on a show like this!

Snapping turtles are known in scientific terms as *Chelydra serpentina*. *Chelydra* refers to the shells (carapaces) they wear on their backs; *serpentina* to their snake-like tails, often as long as the carapace itself. They are actually fresh water turtles, but they seem to do quite well in the brackish creeks and inlets along the coast. In fact, they manage to survive in all kinds of environments, as long as there is water. Their range extends from Canada to South America, from the Atlantic Coast to the Rocky Mountains. They are still fairly common over most of their range.

The snapping turtle's most notable characteristic is its pugnacity. Ernest Thompson Seton described it as "the strongest for its size and the fiercest of all reptiles," gazing on the world with "tiny wicked eyes." It is the villain in his 1911 novel *Rolf in the Woods*, engaging in a vicious battle with the hero. Actually, while snappers are indeed voracious predators, most aggressive behavior they show toward humans is in self-defense. Snappers have a reduced carapace, or top shell, and an even smaller plastron, or lower shell, which means they have less protection than most turtles. This may be the reason they display such an aggressive attitude to those who approach them on land. Under water, where they can move quickly and escape, they are much less aggressive.

There is no denying the appetite of the snapper, however. They will eat just about anything; from algae and duckweed to shrimp, frogs, small mammals, and ducks. Snapping turtle eggs and hatchlings are preyed upon by snakes, herons, and raccoons, but full-sized snappers have few enemies except for humans. Snapping turtle meat has been a popular food since the days when the Native Americans claimed this land. The colonists added it to their diet, and there continues to be a market for it today. The original *Ocracoke Cookbook*, published by the United Methodist Women a number of years ago, has an island recipe for stewed snapping turtle cooked with potatoes, onions, and wine. I can't say, however, remembering those two leathery, roughshod reptiles, that they looked especially appetizing to me.

The display Calvin and I witnessed was a fascinating moment of natural history, but it was only part of the story. The true miracle takes place later: the development of new life within the female; the depositing of 20 to 60 leathery, ovoid eggs in a nest she digs on land; the hatching of these eggs two to three months later into perfect miniature snapping turtles. This is the miracle of springtime, the miracle of life.

I wonder if, come fall, I will see some of the tiny offspring scooting around in the creek or hiking across my yard. Perhaps they will disappear into the obscurity of the dark muddy waters, not to be seen again until another spring entices them to the surface to recreate the miracle of life.

The unpopular sea nettles

June was here again, and it was time to vacate my house and open it for rentals. I was sorry to be leaving Marsh Haven, but I was immensely excited about the upcoming summer. My friend Don and I were preparing to sail south on Aurora, *his 28-foot sailboat. We had spent two previous summers sailing on the Chesapeake Bay in Virginia and Maryland, but this would be a new experience for me. I had already taken my cats Scamp and Squirt to Richmond to spend the summer with their "grandparents" (my folks). Huck and Miss Kelley would come with us. I had bought them their own life preservers and harnesses, and we had been giving Huck swimming lessons. We had ferried them out in the kayaks to the sailboat, where they were getting used to being "swabbies." We finished making our last-minute preparations, gave Marsh Haven one final cleaning, then prepared to say goodbye to Ocracoke for the summer.*

"Oh, you don't have to worry about getting stung around here. We have very few stinging nettles at Ocracoke," I blithely assured Sara, as we discussed the possibility of a swim in Pamlico Sound.

She, her husband Doug Hunt, and their son, Elliot, distant relatives from Colorado, were staying at my house for a week as I prepared to set sail for the summer. Her face expressed doubt.

"Well, I'm pretty sure Elliot and I got stung yesterday," she said.

"I doubt it," I said, trying to reassure her. "There are tons of nettles up in the Chesapeake Bay, but I don't know that I've ever been stung by one here."

Just goes to show you should never act as if you know it all. That very afternoon, as I paddled my kayak across the harbor to the sailboat, I looked down and saw myriads of translucent, be-ribboned globs of jelly drifting beneath me. Sara was right. The waters of Ocracoke had been invaded by an army of stinging nettles.

Sea nettles, as they are also called, (*Chrysaora quinquecirrha*) are one of the *Scyphozoans*, or "cap animals." Known more commonly as jellyfish, Scyphozoans are not fish at all, but belong to the phylum *Coelenterata*, along with the corals, sea anemones, and sea fans. All are aquatic and must live in marine environments. They are invertebrates and are characterized by radial (circular) symmetry.

Jellyfish have an umbrella-shaped cap and a central stalk, both of which are made of a jelly-like translucent substance which is 90 percent water. The cap contains a layer of muscular tissue, which produces an opening and closing motion and results in a slow form of locomotion. Along the margins of the cap are a series of small organs sensitive to light that serve as primitive eyes. Attached to the cap's outer rim are tentacles, and it is these tentacles that can, depending on the species, create havoc among human swimmers and fishermen. Along each tentacle are thousands of cell structures called nematocysts, used by the jellyfish to capture their prey. These contain barbed, harpoon-like threads, often coated with toxic proteins, which are ejected through tiny trap doors when stimulated by physical contact. If that contact is with a human, and if the species is a sea nettle, the result is a very unhappy camper who may be cursing or crying with pain.

If, on the other hand, the victim is a copepod, fish larva, or other member of the zooplankton that floats in the sea (which no doubt the jellyfish would much prefer) the result is dinner for the jellyfish. The toxins paralyze the prey and the tentacles direct it to the mouth, a large opening in the central stalk. From there, it passes to the stomach, where it is rapidly digested, and out through the gut wall cells into the rest of the body.

Jellyfish are considered to be simple, rather primitive life forms. They have neither brain nor heart, but they have an incredibly complicated reproductive system. They recreate by both sexual and asexual methods, known as "alternation of generations." Adult males propel sperm into the water, which then enter the mouths of the females and fertilize the eggs located there. The eggs develop into tiny larvae called planula, each covered with hair-like cilia that help them swim. They are ejected from the female and after a few days settle to the bottom and attach to a hard object. They transform into polyps,

which as they eat and grow through the winter, produce buds. The buds also develop into polyps. In the spring, a strange process called strobilization turns all the polyps into a stack of disks. Each disk breaks off, grows tentacles, and becomes an ephrya. The

ephrya, now in what is known as the medussa stage, grow into jelly-fish. In the case of stinging nettles, this final process takes place in June. By mid-September they have died, leaving behind a new generation of developing polyps.

About 200 kinds of jellyfish live in the oceans of the world. The waters around Ocracoke are home to a number of species, including the harmless moon jelly, the lion's mane (seen in the spring), and the sometimes dangerous Portuguese man-o-war, not a true jellyfish but a close relative.

Stinging nettles can be distinguished from other species by their tentacles, which may be up to two feet in length, by four long frilly mouth lips on the underside of the cap, and by stripes radiating from the center of the translucent cap's topside. Adults can be up to eight inches in diameter.

Unpopular as they are among humans, nettles have their place in nature. They are a favorite food for sea turtles and giant ocean sun-fish, which seem to be resistant to their stings. They provide refuge for several species of fish and crabs, which escape their enemies by hiding in the tentacles. Harvestfish use them as homes while young; then the ingrates consume them for dinner when they grow up.

Nettles got their name in the 1600s from early colonists, according to Dr. Kent Mountford, because their sting brought skin irritation similar to that caused by a common European plant by that name. Dr. Mountford relates a story from the *Maryland Gazette* in 1750 about an Annapolis man who "became entangled in a great number of sea-nettles and was drowned" (perhaps from an allergic reaction?). A "Jellyfish Act" was passed by Congress in the 1960s, setting aside money for research on getting rid of the aggravating creatures. But ecologists Bob Ulanowicz and Don Baird, who work at the Chesapeake Bay Biological Laboratory, believe that human activities may be increasing, not decreasing, sea nettle populations. They speculate that the nutrient overload pouring into coastal waters from sewage systems and farming activities may be causing a proliferation of jellyfish just as it causes a decline in oysters, fish, and many other species.

Whether we humans like them or not, we owe jellyfish some respect. They have been around for 500 million years, according to Dr. Dorothy Spangenberg, and were our first multi-cellular animals. Not only that, they were among the first "astronauts." Baby jellyfish rode the space shuttles in 1991 and 1994 as part of an experiment on how low gravity affects earth creatures.

Worthiness of respect notwithstanding, the scarcity of sea nettles was one of the aspects I particularly enjoyed about the beaches in North Carolina. In fact, it was one of the reasons my friend Don and I had decided to sail south this summer rather than return to Chesapeake Bay, where I'd had unpleasant encounters with them. We were surprised at the numbers of sea nettles we saw as we sailed out of the channel into Pamlico Sound.

At nearby Beaufort, one of our first ports, I called a biologist at the Institute of Marine Sciences to ask about the surprising appearance of the nettles. As it turned out, several interns from Marine Fisheries had just returned from the Outer Banks and had wondered about it too.

The biologist explained that summer jellyfish, as he called them, usually live in the less saline waters near the mainland. A westerly wind, however, had been blowing for several days, and it had pushed the jellyfish east toward the barrier islands. They would not survive long in the salty environment, but in the meantime they could aggravate a lot of swimmers and fishermen at Ocracoke. In fact, even after death the tentacles could still sting if touched.

So I won't be telling anyone else not to worry about sea nettles at Ocracoke, at least not until I've checked out the wind direction. And maybe I'll buy a supply of meat tenderizer, which is reputed to lessen the pain of the sting. But even a few stings from jellyfish are a small price to pay for all the joy to be found at Ocracoke.

Cruising with dolphins

Huck and Miss Kelley took a few days to get used to sailing, but then we settled into a comfortable daily routine. One of our biggest challenges, we soon found, was finding places where we could anchor and walk Huck. After a swift and rough passage across Pamlico Sound, we started following the Intra-coastal Waterway at Oriental, taking our time and visiting the little towns that lined its banks.

At Snow's Cut, near the mouth of the Cape Fear River, we found ourselves directly in the path of a huge storm, Hurricane Bertha. We took refuge at a small marina and spent several frightening days holed up there. We hunkered in the cabin, hatches closed tightly, as 100-mile-per-hour winds battered the area. Later we joined a handful of other boaters who had chosen to ride out the storm and shared rations for the next two days while stores were closed and the town was under curfew. Luckily, we escaped without damage and after a few days we were again on our way.

We spent most of the summer cruising and exploring; passing along the banks of old indigo farms, watching anhingas, wood storks, and bald eagles through our binoculars, docking for a few days in historic Charleston. We followed little-known rivers until they became too shallow for our draft, then continued on in our kayaks, finding ourselves face-to-face with seemingly benign American alli-

gators and occasional ill-tempered water snakes. We ran aground a few times but we always managed to get back on our way. Finally, when we reached the Georgia border we turned around and headed back home to Ocracoke.

My paddle blade slid smoothly through the dark water as I propelled the kayak forward, using a consistent motion that was rhythmic and relaxing. Huck sat between my knees, watching everything with bright-eyed expectation. We were traveling across part of St. Helena Sound, riding the gentle waves that were kicked up by the wake of passing boats.

Suddenly, without warning, the water exploded beside us and a large grey shape emerged, giving us a brief glimpse of two big eyes and a rounded beak. It disappeared, but a minute or so later rose again, still beside us, not more than a foot or so from the kayak.

I felt Huck tremble with excitement and in a low voice I told him to sit still as I continued to paddle. Although startled, I tried to remain calm; but in truth I was thrilled.

I recognized our companion as a bottle-nose dolphin, one of the friendliest of aquatic mammals. I had never had a dolphin swim so close to me, and this one was obviously enjoying the visit. He rose again in front of us, then on the other side. By now, however, Huck was beside himself, and I could not prevent him from expressing his excitement in a loud, sharp bark.

That was it. Our delphic friend dipped out of sight. A minute later, however, a short distance away, we saw it leap from the water, arch downward, and disappear with a flick and a smack of its tail.

We were now anchored near Beaufort, South Carolina, but we

had been watching dolphins on our entire cruise south. We had watched them feeding and playing in the waves and had heard the hoarse rasp of their "blows" as they came to the surface to breathe. Occasionally we had enjoyed the company of especially friendly or curious individuals who swam with us, surfacing beside and around *Aurora* as she skimmed before the wind.

Atlantic bottlenose dolphins (*Tursiops truncatus*) are the best known and most prolific of the marine mammals living in the coastal waters of the Carolinas. The television series "Flipper" has made bottlenose dolphins into a household word, and their performances are always among the most popular shows at aquariums and theme parks. They are not to be confused with the dolphin fish, which bear the same name but are an entirely unrelated animal. Nor are they the same as porpoises, a related but distinctly different family by whose name they are sometimes called. Porpoises are generally smaller than dolphins, lack the beak-like snouts, have more fused cervical vertebrae, and are shyer around humans.

Dolphins and porpoises are actually small whales, or Cetaceans. They belong to the sub-order *Odontoceti* or "toothed whales," along with the sperm and killer whales. Dolphins, or *Delphinidae*, reach an average length of from eight to 10 feet and weigh somewhere between 300 and 650 pounds, with males generally larger than females. They can live for 40 years or more.

Only humans have larger brains than dolphins. While this is not necessarily a measure of intelligence, many people believe dolphins to be extremely smart. They use tools, work cooperatively with other cetaceans and humans, and demonstrate long-term memory and reasoning power in tests.

They communicate through a series of whistles and squeals which they make by forcing air through their blowholes. Scientists believe that each dolphin has a distinctive voice by which other dolphins recognize it. A series of clicks, known as echolocation is used to locate food and to navigate. This complex system is similar to sonar.

Highly socialized animals, dolphins travel in small groups known as pods and sometimes gather in herds of several hundred. They band together to surround and corner the fish they eat, driving them into shallow water or even up onto the shore. Female dolphins with newly born calves are often accompanied by another dolphin, an "auntie," which can be male or female, and which helps in taking care of the calf.

Dolphins apparently do not form monogamous ties between males and females, but male dolphins often have strong friendships with other males. Besides traveling and fishing together, they work cooperatively to herd females, often against their wishes. Females form looser friendships and sometimes try to protect or hide other females from the males.

Many stories tell of dolphins helping other dolphins and whales, even risking their lives for them. When one is sick or injured other dolphins will carry it to the surface, supporting it so it can breathe, and will continue this service until it either dies or recovers.

Bottlenose dolphins are probably best known for their friendliness toward human beings. Mythology and history are full of stories of dolphins rescuing shipwrecked sailors or leading lost ships to port. In one Greek legend Arion escaped a mutiny by his crew by playing a tune on his lyre and leaping into the sea. He was rescued by a dolphin who heard his song. The Roman writer Pliny related the story of a boy who was saved by a dolphin and carried to safety on its back, and Raphael, the great artist of the Italian Renaissance, sculpted a statue depicting the event in 1500. Dolphins have saved more than one human swimmer from attacking sharks, and they are used today in therapeutic sessions to help disturbed children.

If you spend much time at the beach at Ocracoke you are sure to see dolphins out beyond the breakers; riding the waves, chasing fish, and just having a good time. Despite their seeming abundance, however, they are considered a "depleted" species by the National Marine Fisheries Service. A mysterious disease wiped out half the Atlantic coastal stock in 1987-88, and it is believed that fewer than 12,000, perhaps as few as 2,000, live along our coast today. It is feared that they may even now be accumulating man-made toxins such as PCBs (polychlorinated biphenyls) and TBT (tributyltin) which suppress their immune systems and affect their navigational abilities. If so, another major die-off is a distinct possibility. We surely owe it to our friends the dolphins (as well as to other marine life) to take the necessary measures to eliminate these chemical killers in our waters.

It was no doubt a proof of the good will between dolphins and humans that I felt absolutely no fear when the dolphin appeared next to my kayak. I couldn't help but wonder, however, how it felt about dogs. I had noticed before that the dolphins that surfaced near the sailboat always disappeared if Huck barked. The one who swam beside my kayak seemed to be quite offended by the sound. I wondered if they were afraid of dogs, or if the noise hurt or disturbed their hearing organs. Perhaps Huck had said something that was positively rude; something I did not understand but which the dolphin found highly insulting. Whatever the reason, it was the end of our camaraderie. Next time I go dolphin-watching I will leave Huck at home, or at least insist that he keep his mouth shut.

The case of the missing
sand dollars

Back home again, I settled into a comfortable routine. I began working 30 hours a week at the Fig Tree, a bakery/delicatessen owned by my friend Carol Beach. The work was diversified and fun. I made sandwiches and soups, baked a little, and handled the register. I could get there on my bicycle, and I still had time to work on some of the projects I wanted to do around the house. My father had, over the past few years, bequeathed to me part of his tool collection: hammer, saws, drill, square, level, etc. He had shown me how to use them when I was a child, engaging in joint ventures to create doll furniture, stick horses, and lizard cages. Growing up, I helped him build and repair the fences and gates which subdivided our 15-acre farm. Later still I assisted my (then) husband Pete in his work as a mobile home repairman. After moving to Marsh Haven I was bound and determined to do my own carpentry work, albeit with the help of friends.

Now I took out Daddy's tools again. I measured and cut boards, re-measured and re-cut, nailed them together, pulled out nails and re-nailed. I sported a purple thumb for a few weeks and learned a set of epithets that would make a sailor proud. It usually took me two or three tries to get things right (well, close to right) but when I finished I was immensely proud of my new porch steps, fence, and other *projects. And even after all my nail pounding, I still had plenty of opportunities to kayak and go to the beach.*

The waters of Pamlico Sound shimmered like the ripples in an antique mirror as I drove my truck onto a high stretch of hard sand and turned off the engine. Don and I were at South Point, the southwest tip of Ocracoke where the Atlantic Ocean meets the estuary, connected by a channel of deep, swift water known as Ocracoke Inlet.

From where we sat we could see a fishing trawler heading back through the inlet toward the Creek, its outriggers up and its hold presumably full of flounder. If we turned and looked behind us, back up the island, we could see the continuous but irregular flash of whitecaps as long, rolling ocean waves broke on underwater shoals as they neared the shore. The waves grew calmer at the point, and here great black-backed and herring gulls waded in the shallows. An array of broken whelk shells and bits of driftwood stretched across the sand that spanned the distance from the ocean to where we had parked near the sound.

We had not come to beachcomb or birdwatch. We had a mission. We untied our kayaks from the top of the truck, dragged them to the western side of the point, pushed off, and paddled into the sound. We were headed for Sand Dollar Island.

Sand Dollar Island is not a real island. Most of the time it is underwater. It is a reef of sand that lies a few hundred feet offshore, with conditions that apparently make perfect habitat for the flat, silver-dollar-shaped echinoderms we call sand dollars. I had often found the bleached out "tests," or exoskeletons, of dead sand dollars that had washed up on the nearby beach. Locals had told me that they came from an underwater sandbar, and that if you went there at low tide, when the top of the bar creeped above the water line, you could find dozens of them. Don had been there the year before with his friend Dave Isner and verified this. He and Dave had brought back handfuls. Now Don was going to let me see for myself.

The animals we were looking for are not, technically speaking, sand dollars at all. They are keyhole urchins, known by the scientific name *Mellita quinquiesperforata*. They have several keyhole shaped openings in their bodies, which give them their common name. True Atlantic sand dollars live north of the mid-Atlantic and are seldom found along the coast here. The technicality in naming, however, seems arbitrary, and almost everyone knows them as sand dollars.

Keyhole urchins are among the most familiar and popular finds of beachcombers who search for treasures along the Mid-Atlantic coast beaches. Close relatives to the similar but thicker sea biscuits and sea urchins, they belong, along with sea stars and sea cucumbers, to the phylum Echinodermata, which is Greek for "hedgehog skin." Most echinoderms possess a spiny outer coating that protects them and gives them their name.

Sand dollars have a rigid outer shell, the test, formed of calcareous skeletal plates, or ossicles, which are fused together. This shell is covered with tiny movable spines which give the animals a smooth felt-like texture and a yellow-brown color. The top, or aboral, side of the sand dollar has a five-petal pattern which corresponds to the five rays of its cousin the sea star and the five rows of tube feet of the sea urchin. Most of the sand dollars found along the beaches are dead and have lost their spines. They are bleached to a bright white color upon which the flower-like pattern is easily discernible.

Sometimes known as the Holy Ghost shell, the petals have been described as the Star of Bethlehem, and the slits as the wounds of Christ. Five small "doves of peace" found inside are actually part of the digestive system.

As their name indicates, sand dollars live on sandy bottoms, under which they burrow to escape storms and enemies and to feed. They wave their spines to create currents in the water which move the sand, making it easier for them to burrow under it. Tiny tube feet which extend downward from the five petals are used for respiration, and mucous-covered cilia on the underside of the body collect food in the sand and carry it to the mouth. Here a toothed structure known as Aristotle's lantern helps to ingest the diatoms and other micro-organisms that make up their diet.

Sand dollars are a favorite food of flounders and other bottom fish, making them important residents of Outer Banks waters, not only for the fish that eat them but for the fishermen who catch the fish.

Don and I reached the sand bar with no trouble. We pulled the kayaks onto the sand and looked eagerly around, expecting to see lots of circular white shapes. Instead, we saw only a few brown pelicans resting at the far end of the bar. We walked for a ways but still saw no sand dollars. I remembered that my friend Kathleen O'Neal had said you could find the live ones in the water, under a thin layer of sand. We waded up to our knees, perusing the bottom carefully, feeling for the creatures with our bare feet. Still nothing.

After covering the entire area, above and below water, we finally gave up. The tide was coming in and we were getting cold. Where were the sand dollars? Had the area been silted over? Had the last big storm washed them out? Had pollution from some offshore spill destroyed them?

That was in the fall. I wondered over the winter if Sand Dollar Island was indeed still home to the echinoderms it was named for. Then one day in mid-February a walk on the beach at South Point answered my question. A good blow had hit the day before, and the sand was littered with the silvery white tests, each with its lovely pattern of flower-like petals. They surely must have come from Sand Dollar Island. But where were they on the day we paddled out to search for them?

Goldenrod:
Cinderella of the salt marsh

After years of renting and moving from house to house, I was overjoyed to have my own yard at Marsh Haven. I was as excited about working in the garden as I was about working on the house. I love gardening, a passion I inherited from both my parents. Whenever I pull weeds in my garden, however, I am stricken with a sense of guilt. Weed is such a prejudicial concept, rather like racism in the plant world. I generally find myself muttering apologies as I yank dandelions, pennywort, and unknown intruders from flower beds and lawn. A regular botanical Hitler I am, I tell myself. What's worse, I enjoy the chore, finding it relaxing and therapeutic.

I strive to keep my yard as natural as possible, choosing native plants or those that survive without pesticides, massive doses of fertilizer, or watering. This benefits both me and this fragile environment. I try to work with Mother Nature, but sometimes she pulls a surprise on me.

They first appeared in the springtime, tiny sprigs of green that pushed their way up from last year's roots or burst out of seed husks tossed randomly over the black soil. They were barely noticeable in the profusion of green that sprang forth around my house. Through the summer they grew, becoming lank and spindly lacking any definitive form or color.

Weeds, I thought to myself. *They're blocking the view of the creek and choking out the joebells and broomstraw. I need to clear them out.*

As summer waned, it was obvious that they had developed quite a foothold, not only where they grew beside the creek, but all along the narrow road that leads to my house. They seemed like ungracious intruders as they fought for space with the graceful, whispering marshgrasses. "One of these days," I told myself, "I'll get rid of all these weeds." But it was one of those things I never quite got around to.

A tumultuous summer, rocked by threatening hurricanes and torrential rains, slipped into a quiet and peaceful fall. The marshes changed from soft shades of green to gold and rust. The cedars, which wrap around my windows and porches like a cozy bathrobe, took on a new look. The female, or seed-bearing, trees turned a soft blue, adorning themselves with berries that would feed the winter birds and spawn new saplings in the spring. When the sun fell upon them in early morning or at dusk, they created a harmonious contrast with the dark evergreen boughs of their male, or pollen-bearing, counterparts.

Along the branches of the wax myrtle, or bayberry trees, small baby blue fruit appeared, attracting the graceful, fluttering myrtle warblers as they made their way south for the winter. Woven in among the myrtle and the cedar, the shiny dark leaves of the yaupon holly were bejewelled with berries as well, green now in fall, but bearing the promise of turning bright shades of red when the cold of winter came. The colors of fall were as soft in the marsh as the quiet progression of the season.

The transition must have taken place gradually, over a period of days, but to me it didn't seem that way. I awoke one October morning and looking outside, found myself surrounded by a curtain of yellow fire, as if the brightest rays of the sun had come to earth, enveloping me and my house. The plain, awkward-looking weeds, unwanted trespassers in my marsh haven, had been visited, it seemed, by a fairy godmother. Like the poor stepchild Cinderella, they had donned new clothes and burst into beauty, turning my little piece of Ocracoke into a bright and cheery ballroom.

"Goldenrod," I told myself in amazement. My unwanted "weeds" were seaside goldenrod, one of the island's most colorful wildflowers. How grateful I was that my laziness had prevented me from pulling them. *Solidago sempervirens*, as this flower is known in scientific terms, is a member of the daisy family. It is one of almost 100 varieties of goldenrod found in North America, most in the eastern

United States. It is a perennial herb with an erect, fibrous stem, creeping roots, and fleshy, basal, toothed leaves that grow along the stem. The bright yellow flowers are small and fragrant, arranged in groups along the stem. Seeds, cradled in soft gray-white down, appear after the flowering, but most propagation is through new growth that comes up from the roots. Contrary to common belief, goldenrod does not cause hay fever. The heavy pollen is not airborne, but carried by insects. It is ragweed, which blooms at the same time, that causes the sneezing and nose-blowing.

According to my guide to Indian herbology of North America, goldenrod can be eaten in a salad, used as an external lotion for wounds and sores, and makes a delicious herbal tea which helps cure upset stomachs and colds. I had to try it. I picked a few handfuls of the leaves and yellow blossoms and placed them on a tray in my oven, where the gas-fueled pilot light would provide a steady warm temperature. Two days later it was ready for my friend Sandy Wright and me to taste.

I crumbled a spoonful and placed it in my teaball, a handy contraption for brewing leaf tea. I dropped the teaball into a mug, filled it with boiling water, and left it to steep for a few minutes. We agreed that with a little sugar it tasted quite good, but since we were feeling quite healthy I was unable to pass judgment on its medicinal qualities.

For a week I was surrounded by the spectacular yellow blooms. Butterflies appeared to feed on them, engaging in a last pre-winter orgy as they drank the sweet wine of the blossoms. Goldenrod is the primary food of migrating monarchs, and hosts of them stopped to partake of the banquet as they prepared for their long trip to Mexico.

The colorful panorama has dulled now. The blossoms have fallen to the ground, and the goldenrod has again taken on a rather messy appearance, shedding fuzzy grayish seed pods as the green stalks turn a dull brown. But it had its moment in the sun, and it taught me a lesson. Next year, instead of casting thoughts of aspersion on it, I'll learn to enjoy it, borrowing a few leaves for tea, trying a few more in a salad. And I'll look forward to that short week in fall when it surrounds my home with a halo of gold and invites butterflies to partake of its nectar of life.

Marsh Haven Enterprises

I can not remember a time in my life when I did not have at least one cat. One of my favorite memories of summer in Short Pump, Virginia, where I grew up, was climbing up to the top of the hay pile where Black Fur had her kittens and curling up in contentment next to their warm velveteen bodies. The first kitten I had of my own, Princess, was killed by a car when I was seven. Tiny, our St. Bernard dog, found her and carried her home, cradling her gently in her mouth. Later my parents got me Tiger Lily, and she ruled the house thereafter until the ripe old age of 21. My cat Scamper is her great-granddaughter.

The cats I had as a child roamed freely. But as I grew up I witnessed over and over the damage that cats could do to birds and other small animals and that automobiles could do to cats. As a result I decided to enforce a strict rule in my life: all cats indoors. What's more, I did not want to have any more cats than could live with me in harmony and peace. Two seemed like a good number. As I watched other Ocracoke residents gather in the strays I remained firm; I would help in spaying them, finding them homes, treating the sick or injured ones. But I would NOT adopt them.

As I settled into Marsh Haven that second fall, however, I was faced with a dilemma. I discovered that while I was gone a small colony of scared but very hungry wild cats had moved into the neighborhood. I watched them slink around the perimeters of my yard, raiding the garbage and eating any small live creature they could catch. They drove Huck crazy, and he in turn drove me crazy with his barking. This wouldn't do.

Unhappy as I was about their presence, I didn't want to hurt them. I decided the only action I could take would be to place the kittens in homes, and spay and neuter the adults so that there would not be even more next year. That, I knew, was easier said than done. First, I would have to catch them. So I began feeding them and, in the process, found myself falling in love with them. Over the next few months I accomplished my goals, finding homes for the four kittens (one particularly wild one now sleeps in my parents' bed) and neutering all the adults. The trouble was, whether I liked it or not, Marsh Haven was now their home.

They have lived on my deck ever since, and though I have managed to find homes for a few, new ones always seem to show up to replace them. With the help of my friends, who feed them when I'm gone, they stay fat and sassy and, surprisingly, kill very few birds. In the three years that they have been here I have found evidence of only one avian casualty. They are now, along with the birds, an important part of my life.

"All right guys, breakfast!" I was standing on the deck beside my house, wrapped in a checked flannel bathrobe and bedroom slippers, shivering as I divvied out a half quart of dry cat food into bowls.

Thomas, a big bulls-eye yellow tabby, immediately plopped on top of one bowl, stretching his front legs spread-eagled across the food so no one else could get his head in. The others were more polite. Sweet Pea and Boots shared one bowl. Midnight, Half Moon, and Jezebel took turns at another, while Buddy ate from a pile on the wooden plank. Mosby, too timid or polite to stand up for himself, had a bowl on the walkway.

Giving each a pat on the head, I hurried to the front of the house, peeked over the edge of the bird feeder hanging from the cedar tree and, finding it almost empty, scooped a cupful of mixed birdseed out of the tin container on the porch and filled it.

Then I went into the house, removed a bag of finger mullet from the refrigerator, and hand-fed three to the injured loon who resided in a cage on the side of my porch. Retreating back to the kitchen, I gave my three indoor cats and my dog each a handful of dry food, poured myself a cup of hot coffee, and pulled up a chair in front of the fire. The first chores of the day were done.

In winter, Ocracoke sheds its tourist trappings; restaurants close; cold winds blow; and sometimes nor'easters and flooding stop the ferries and close the roads. Some Ocracokers close up their houses and head for warmer or more exciting environs. A lot of us stay, however. Outsiders often ask what on earth we do during those long lonely months. We bundle up in warm clothes and rubber boots, surround ourselves with books or videos, and pursue whatever passions we particularly enjoy.

As for myself, I stay very busy running the Marsh Haven Kitty Kafe on the side deck of my house. The clientele consists of eight to 10 "regulars," a motley crew of tabbies, tortoiseshells, oranges, blacks, and grays, plus their guests. We are open for breakfast and dinner. The menu is simple, featuring such entrees as our "9 Lives Tuna Felini," "G. Whiskers Chicken Plate," and our most popular "Purina Platter." I also run occasional specials, such as "Turkey Skin Supreme" and "Leftover Bluefish Blitz."

Meals are free except for one slight fee: all diners are required to get spayed or neutered. I work for tips, which include purrs, leg rubbings, and adoring looks. My three indoor cats, Scamp, Squirt, and Miss Kelley have observation privileges from the porch; and Huck, my doberman, insists on barking privileges, even though it is against restaurant rules.

I also continue to operate Marsh Haven Avian Eatery, a diverse restaurant offering a variety of culinary choices and dining settings geared to the taste of our winged customers. I have the usual cuisine of sunflower, thistle seeds, and mixed birdseed, available in three cozy rooms, all decorated in the latest "Birdfeeder" styles. These are preferred by suburban customers, such as the cardinals, finches, and jays. In "The Creek" dining area "catch-your-own" fresh fish, crab, and shrimp are offered for the seafood loving crowd (the herons,

kingfishers, grebes, and cormorants); and on the second story is "The Boughery," where specialties include juicy cedar berries, melt-in-your-mouth yaupon berries, and crunchy wax myrtle berries, all served in a tasteful decor of verdant leaves with comfortable branch seating. These delicacies are preferred by some of my more discriminating customers, such as the cedar waxwings, Carolina wrens, and a variety of warblers. The pelicans, marsh hawks, and an occasional osprey dine in the nearby salt marsh and sound, and while I enjoy watching them from my bedroom window as they enjoy their repast, they seldom choose to mingle with our crowd. Once again, my salary is minimal, but there are fringe benefits, such as not having to go to movie theaters, video arcades, or rowdy bars for entertainment.

Marsh Haven Bed and Band-aid™, my small wildlife rehabilitation center for ailing birds and other critters, is less entertaining and can often be heart-breaking. It is not a full-time operation, but keeps me busy when the wards are full. It is supported by donations from concerned residents and tourists and operates within the regulations required by my state and federal licenses. Many of my patients are among the varied species of gulls, but I also treat loons, herons, pelicans, cormorants, grebes, mergansers, brants, gannets, chuckwill's-widows, and all kinds of songbirds; even an occasional glass snake, snapping turtle, or harbor seal. I have yet to see a patient that

carried Blue Cross or Medicare, so again the rewards are not monetary. It is worth it, however, when you can release a bird that otherwise would have died, and watch it soar away into the sky or dive into the depths of Pamlico Sound, happy and free.

So when folks want to know if I get bored in the winter I answer with an emphatic, "Not likely." Ocracoke offers all the entertainment I need in winter.

The humble menhaden

I had, as usual, gone home to Virginia for Christmas Day, and was now back at Ocracoke, trying to stay warm and employed. The Fig Tree, along with most island businesses, was closed for the winter, so I was refinishing furniture and caning chairs whenever the work was available. I also resumed picking, drying, and packaging yaupon tea.

Calls about injured wildlife came in as usual. A ring-billed gull had been hit by a car and its wing hopelessly mangled (it had to be put to sleep.) A tri-colored heron was trapped in one of the canals, unable to fly away (I took off my shoes, rolled up my pants, and, using clippers and gloves, released it from the tangle of grass that held it.) A glass snake (a kind of legless lizard) was accidentally unearthed from its winter underground sleep at a construction site (I re-buried it in an aquarium, to be released in spring.) A myrtle warbler had crashed into a glass window at the post office (I kept it in a warm box for a day until it recovered from the shock and trauma.) A young seal was found injured and near death on the beach (it died as I administered subcutaneous fluids.) My rehab work was often upsetting, sometimes depressing; but it was never boring!

It was cold, freezing cold, as I crept into the darkness, and I was startled when the heavy door swung shut behind me. I hurried back to make sure that I was not locked in and felt relief when it opened to my touch.

Still, thoughts swirled in my head about those television horror films where the lock was stealthily turned on the freezer door and the victim was found frozen stiff the next morning. I was in the freezer room at the South Point Fish House on the Creek. To make things even more macabre, I clutched in my hand a huge cleaver-like knife.

I advanced carefully across the cold cement floor to my destination—a giant pile of fish. Their beady frozen eyes stared up at me through the dim light, making me feel vaguely guilty as I began hacking them loose from their frozen comrades. It was so unbearably cold that I had to take several breaks to rush outside and warm up. Finally I had what I had come for; a bag of quick-frozen Atlantic menhaden, known more often at Ocracoke as fatbacks.

I stepped outside and pulled the door behind me, rubbing my arms to restore circulation. I thanked Vernon Smith, a friend who worked at the fish house. He grinned at me as I trotted down the steps and climbed on my bicycle, fish in hand. "Tell Murray thanks," I called as I pedaled away.

This was not the first time I had come to the South Point Fish House for menhaden. Murray Fulcher, the owner, had been generously supplying me with fish for the water birds at Marsh Haven, my wildlife rehabilitation clinic, for several years. The ones I had today were for a brown pelican whose wing had been entangled and cut by a fishing line. I preferred to take home fresh fish brought in the same day by the commercial fishermen, but fishing had been bad that week so I had to fall back on the old standby, frozen menhaden. The pelican did not like it as much as fresh fish, but at least it wouldn't starve.

Atlantic menhaden (*Brevoortia tyrannus*) are not a big sport fish like tuna or dolphin. They are not a popular dining choice such as

flounder or Spanish mackerel, served in first class restaurants. Not many people eat them at all these days. They are, however, some of the most important fish along the Atlantic coast. They provide food for all kinds of larger fish and for pelicans, loons, ospreys, and other fish-eating birds, as well as for bottlenose dolphins and harbor seals. As the most abundant and available prey, they are an essential part of the food chain and the ecology of the Eastern Seaboard, according to Greg Garman, Director of the Center for Environmental Studies at Virginia Commonwealth University.

Although unpleasing to the human palate, they also have great economic importance. They are ground and used for a number of purposes, such as chicken food and fertilizer. The name "menhaden" is, in fact, derived from the Indian word for fertilizer or manure. Ranging all the way from Nova Scotia to Florida, they go by such nicknames as pogis, alewives, bugfish, bunkers, greentails, and the name Ocracokers use, fatbacks.

Relatively small fish, maturing at about 14 inches, they are silver colored with brassy sides, dark bluish-green backs, and numerous spots on their sides. Long, closely set gill rakers allow them to filter out the plankton which forms much of their diet. They belong to the family of bony fish known as *clupeidai*, or herrings, which are highly specialized schooling fish with primitive origins. There are three other species of menhaden, one of which, the yellow fin, occasionally inhabits North Carolina waters. None share the economic or ecological importance of the Atlantic menhaden.

Adult menhaden travel in shallow coastal waters in schools that may number more than 100,000. They spawn at the edge of the continental shelf south of Hatteras in the winter, depending on favorable winds and currents to carry their eggs and larvae to sounds and bays. From there they swim up the creeks to brackish waters and tidal marshes, where for about six months they feed and grow. These juveniles then gradually move back into the sounds where they continue to grow until reaching sexual maturity, at about three or four years. They then join other adult menhaden as they swim along the Atlantic coastal waters.

Some scientists believe that because menhaden eat a large amount of algae they play an important part in maintaining the health of ocean and sound waters. Excess algae depletes the water of oxygen as it decays, causing fish kills and other environmental degradation. Menhaden in the Chesapeake Bay also consume, according to studies, approximately nine percent of the nitrogen, a nutrient that is, along with phosphorus, one of the worst pollutants of coastal waters.

Menhaden have had a place in American history since early times. Thomas Morton described in 1632 how Indians in Virginia fertilized their fields with them, using 1,000 fish per acre and increasing their yield of corn threefold. They apparently were popular as a food fish in colonial times. William Byrd wrote the following in 1737:

"Fatbacks. This is a small but very good fish, as fat as butter and is a splendid fish when baked." As late as 1874 they sold, according to George Brown Goode's *History of the American Menhaden*, in Washington D.C. for almost as much as its most popular fish, the striped bass or rockfish.

Meanwhile, another use for the plentiful little fish had been discovered. Sometime around 1811 Christopher Barker and John Tallman of Rhode Island extracted oil by boiling menhaden in a pot. They skimmed the oil off and placed it in barrels, thus sowing the seeds for a new industry. The fatty ridge on the back of the fish (from which the name "fatback" derives) produced a high concentration of oil, which could be used instead of whale oil for lighting. Harvesting soon began in earnest, by means of gill nets, haul seines, and purse nets.

Today electricity has replaced the need for fuel oil, but menhaden are still harvested for fertilizer and animal feed. At one time menhaden factories operated from Maine to Florida, but only two still exist on the East Coast. The factory at Reedville, Virginia, established in 1867 by Captain Elijah Reed, is the largest, with a fleet of thirteen vessels. A smaller factory at Beaufort, North Carolina, has three ships.

The fishing ships use spotter planes to locate the menhaden, which form a dark shadow in the water. Two small boats surround the school with a large net, known as a purse seine. When the net is set, the mother ship uses a winch to gradually draw the net into a tight bowl, or "purse," beside the ship. The fish are dipped out and dropped into the ship's hold.

Between them, the factories at Reedville and Beaufort caught and processed 263,000 metric tons of menhaden in 1997. The annual catch of menhaden in the United States is 400,000 tons, making it the third largest fishery, by weight, in the country.

The harvesting of menhaden is a controversial enterprise today. Sports fishermen complain that heavy commercial harvesting negatively impacts such gamefish as blues and striped bass, which depend on them for food. Biologists worry that over-harvesting will deplete these and other natural predators, such as loons and bald eagles, which also depend on them. Tourist businesses on the Outer Banks say that menhaden fishing ships, which operate close to swimming and fishing beaches, are bad for tourism. Efforts to limit how close menhaden ships can come to shore are underway.

Niels Moore of the National Fisheries Institute says that menhaden is a highly resilient species well able to survive current fishing pressures. "They go through wide swings in abundance due to environmental conditions," says Greg Garman of Virginia Commonwealth University. "If other conditions are optimal, they should not be harmed by commercial harvesting. But in bad years, any additional pressures, such as fishing, can make a bad season worse."

The menhaden at South Point Fish House on Ocracoke are not brought in by menhaden ships but by local pound and gill netters, who catch them in Pamlico Sound and sell them to Murray. He, in turn, sells them to crabbers to use as bait, or they are ground up and sold as chum, which is used by fishermen to attract more desirable fish. And, of course, he generously shares some with the ill and injured birds at Marsh Haven.

Many a loon, heron, and pelican flying free owes thanks to South Point Fish House and its frozen menhaden. All of us who love the sea and its inhabitants owe respect and concern for the humble little fish, whose name may mean fertilizer, but whose existence means the well-being of the entire Atlantic Coast ecosystem.

The comet of the century

The month of March, 1997 is inscribed on my memory in indelible, 24-carat gold. An astronomical event that kept scientists glued to their telescopes had a profound effect on me.

Winter was officially ending, though nights were still cold and the island quiet. I took my watercolors out of the closet and began painting again. I hoped to sell a few pieces in Kathleen O'Neal's gallery, the Island Artworks. Toward the end of the month I started working a few hours a week at the Fig Tree Bakery and Deli. I got home in the early evenings, fed the cats and birds, and took Huck for long walks or bicycle rides. Not long after the sun ducked under the horizon I would turn my eyes to the west and lose myself in wonder.

A splash of light riveted my gaze, holding me spellbound as I tried to find some way to verbalize my emotions, but there was none. I thought of the old-fashioned meaning of the word "awful," in the biblical sense, what the dictionary defines as "inspiring reverence, fear, and wonder." "Awe." Yes, that came closest to describing the emotion it inspired in me.

"It," I call it. "The Comet." With all due respect to Hale and Bopp, the two men who discovered it and for whom I have enormous admiration, I can't bring myself to think of it by their names. It seems a bit presumptuous to me, this habit we earthlings have of naming celestial objects after ourselves, as if we were responsible for their existence, merely by pinpointing them with a high-powered telescope.

Hailed as the "comet of the century," it put on one of the most splendid astronomical shows ever witnessed. Everyone had a different reaction to it. One person told me she was disappointed. It didn't live up to the display the press had led her to expect. Someone else said he hadn't even seen it. (How not?) Most people, however, were duly impressed and appreciated the spectacular show we were treated to, free of charge. Some were even as awestruck as I.

It first appeared in the pre-dawn sky, visible only to early risers. Then it moved to prime time, center stage, stealing the show as it spread across the sky. It appeared every night after dusk, and we on the Outer Banks had front row seats, as we do for most night-time sky shows. Few lights dim the clarity, and the view over salt marsh, sound, and sea is unobstructed and dramatic. It was available to everyone, no cable required.

This wasn't the first comet I had seen. The year before I had viewed Hyakutake not only in Ocracoke but from a hilltop in mountainous Asheville. A few years before, in 1988, I had climbed to the observatory outside of Flagstaff, Arizona, and peered through the lens of a giant telescope at the famous Haley's Comet, which steadfastly returns every 76 years. I was intrigued by both sightings, which reawakened my secret, unfulfilled yearnings to be an astronomer.

Comets, scientists believe, are basically balls of rock, dirt, and ice (frozen water, methane, and ammonia) revolving around the sun. When their orbits take them far from the sun, the nucleus becomes inactive, giving off less light. As they move closer to the center of our solar system they are warmed by solar radiation, which releases the gases within the ice. These gases spew forth from the nucleus, carrying dust particles with them, and form an atmosphere around the solid core. This atmosphere, known as the coma (Greek for hair) is what we see as the brilliant head of the comet. Solar winds blow gas and dust back, away from the sun, creating the tail. Fluorescence caused by the sun's radiation creates the light show. As the heated gases escape from the nucleus the comet gradually becomes smaller. Some scientists believe that the escaped gases of comets were the original source of water on earth. Comets may also have brought with them the organic chemicals that formed the origin of life billions of years ago.

Our 1997 dazzler was a giant, with a 25-mile-wide nucleus and a coma of about a million and a half miles. The tail shimmering behind it stretched across more than 100 million miles, approximately the same distance as the comet's closest point to Earth. It will not pass this close again until 4360 AD. If astronomers are correct, it will continue on this orbit, losing more gases each time it nears the sun, until after a thousand trips or so the ice is gone, leaving only a rock core, known as an asteroid, spinning through space.

The science of the comet itself is as fascinating as any spaceship imagined to be following in its wake. But this comet did not speak to the scientist in me. The reverence I felt as I gazed at it was surely akin to religion.

Comets are traditionally thought to be harbingers of doom, embodiments of evil, predictors of the end of the world, but this one spoke to me of hope. It gave me a sense of oneness with the universe and put time and my individual problems into proper perspective.

When it returns again will humans still be here? Who knows?

But it promises a rhythm and continuity not often found in the fast-moving, unpredictable world we have created. What's more, it proves that surprises still await us—unexpected delights that can bring magic into the lives of even the most cynical and information-burdened among us.

While this show, like all others, passed as the comet moved farther from Earth each day, it regaled me for more than a month, adorning the night sky like a splendid jewel on loan from the queen of the universe. As thrilled as I was to see it each evening, I particularly remember a night when I stood gazing across the softly whispering grasses of the marsh past the distant waters of Pamlico Sound, and up through the ebony darkness at the comet thinking, *I will never forget this moment. This night, this memory, will stay with me, wherever I may be, for as long as I live.*

I have only to close my eyes, and I can see The Comet still.

Ocracoke's mystery snake

Spring was here and Ocracoke was beginning to rub its eyes and stretch. Businesses were opening and tourists were arriving. I was trying to attain some proficiency on a pair of roller blades that Barb Adams had traded me, but I wasn't getting far. I tried to practice by myself but occasionally someone would come by as I rolled awkwardly along. I would blithely announce that I was learning to skate, hoping to be told I was doing great. The usual response was a solemn nod accompanied by, "I can tell." As discouraging as that was, I didn't give up.

I was cleaning cottages again and working a few hours a week at Phillip Howard's shop, the Village Craftsman, where I enjoyed the camaraderie of several close friends. I was writing as usual for The Island Breeze and had increased my hours at the Fig Tree. Working at the Fig Tree had several benefits: the pleasures of good company, good food, and a regular paycheck. It also brought my re-introduction to one of Ocracoke's most enigmatic reptilian inhabitants. Carol Beach, the owner, had told me that she used to see small striped snakes behind the bed-and-breakfast next door, but they had not appeared in quite a while. Then one day I heard her call in excitement for me to come outside.

"Come see what's out here!" My friend Carol had her head half-way through the front door of her restaurant, where I was stirring potato salad in the kitchen. She had a trowel in one hand, a basil plant in the other.

She pointed to a large flower pot where I saw a small, worm-like shape that, on closer investigation, proved to be a juvenile snake. It was marked with bands of mottled brown and white. Was it one of Ocracoke's unique kingsnakes? Carol asked. I was sure it was, and we were thrilled and excited.

Looking at it, I was reminded of the winter, six years before, when I had lived at the Sunflower House in Ocracoke Village. That winter I had a special housemate, along with my cats and dog. He didn't help pay the rent, but neither did he create any loud noise or make a mess. Indeed, I didn't know he was there for the first month. Then one day as I trotted down the steps of the porch, my dog Duchess close on my heels, I saw a movement beneath my feet. It was gone in a second, but not before I had time to see the sleek, slithering shape of a snake.

I jumped a foot or so, I must admit. I find snakes extremely interesting and I value them as an important part of our ecosystem; but I'm not wild about coming upon them unexpectedly. Before long the sight of the long lanky reptile became part of the normal routine, however, and Duchess and I accepted its presence as part of the household.

Since I am not a herpetologist and am no expert on snake identification, I looked it up in a reptile guidebook. It appeared to be an eastern kingsnake (*Lampropeltis getulus*), but my snake had white stripes on a dark brown, somewhat speckled background, whereas the snake in the book was black with white stripes. The eastern kingsnake, I read, is a large, sleek, attractive snake with white or yellow stripes. They eat lizards, small mammals, birds, eggs, and other snakes. If caught they may exude a musk-like odor, but are fairly docile when handled.

I never tried to catch or handle the snake living beneath my porch, but it seemed quite comfortable living near me and never showed any hostility. I knew it was not poisonous, and I figured it would seriously discourage any rat or mice boarders who might show up. So regardless of what kind it was, I was happy to have it share my domain.

Since that winter six years ago, I had come across a number of comments, stories, and written accounts of a mysterious snake living at Ocracoke. It was described as an oddly colored kingsnake, and was believed by some to be a sub-species found only on Ocracoke and nearby islands. It had never been formally classified as such, however, and the more I tried to pin down the facts, the more elusive they appeared to be.

Ocracoke Island does not have a great variety of snakes, due to its location, size, and vulnerability to the sea. Those that survive must be able to adapt to the difficult conditions. Only green snakes, black racers, hog-nosed snakes and Carolina salt marsh snakes are common on the island, along, of course, with the unusual looking kingsnakes.

The earliest reference I found to our mystery snake was in a September, 1942, issue of *The American Midland Naturalist* called "Vertebrate Fauna of North Carolina Coastal Islands." In the Ocracoke chapter, University of North Carolina professor William L. Engels describes the snake he found as "strikingly different from typical *getulus* (king snake) in color (chocolate brown), in pattern of coloration on the head, and in the arrangement of rings; it may represent a distinct, hitherto undefined, insular race."

Engels further described the snake in the 1942 *Proceedings of the New England Zoological Club*, explaining how it differed from normal kingsnakes. This snake, he stated, fed almost entirely on mice rather than snakes, and killed them by throwing or pressing them against some solid object, as would a black snake. He suggested that these deviations from normal kingsnake behavior, along with the changes in coloration, exemplify the rapidity with which evolutionary change can take place in isolated instances. He called the snake a new sub-species and named it *sticticeps*.

John Alexander and James Lazell devoted an entire chapter of their book *Ribbon of Sand* to the mysterious snake, which they call the Intercapes kingsnake, referring to the more wind-blown, over-washed sections of the Outer Banks. "In the bizarre case of the Intercapes kingsnake," they wrote, "we scientists stand on an investigative threshold." They described searching for the elusive reptile for years before finally locating it, not on the high ground at Ocracoke where they expected, but in the salt marshes of Portsmouth Island and later Ocracoke. After more years of observation and study, they proposed the theory that these kingsnakes subsist on rice rats, which dwell in chambers and runways beneath large wax myrtle trees; and that the kingsnakes themselves also dwell in these chambers. According to this theory, these snakes are even more highly specialized than Engels had believed, and are an exciting example of Darwinian evolution.

If Alexander and Lazell are right in saying that these snakes live only under myrtle trees in the salt marsh, then the snake I shared housing with could not have been a kingsnake, because there were no large wax myrtle trees around. A number of other Ocracoke residents also recall seeing the oddly marked reptiles, sometimes referred to as Outer Banks Kingsnakes, but not necessarily in salt marshes or under myrtle trees. Carol says a number of them used to live on the dry, sandy lot next to the Fig Tree, but they disappeared after the lot was cleared. Biologist Allen Brelig observed the snakes and confirmed her identification.

Marcia Lyons, naturalist for the Cape Hatteras National Seashore, says that perhaps the snakes move, inhabiting different habitats at different times of the year. She has seen them in brushy areas of Hatteras Island not far from Pamlico Sound.

Not all herpetologists believe that the snake is a separate sub-species. Biologist Richard Blaney has suggested that it is an integrating population with relic genes from Florida, left over from thousands of years ago. The book *Amphibians and Reptiles of the Carolinas and Virginia* remarks on the color differences in the kingsnakes on Ocracoke, but does not refer to them as a unique or separate group.

According to Alvin Brazwell, state herpetologist at the North Carolina Museum of Natural Sciences in Raleigh, "It's been argued back and forth for years. Some would like to list it as a sub-species, others not."

For legal purposes, however, it is listed as a "state special concern sub-species," which means it can't be collected without a permit. After it was identified in the '40s, collectors came in large numbers to capture the snakes and sell them for high dollars. Today permits are only issued if the snakes are to be used for necessary research.

Brazwell believes that the speckling on the kingsnakes at Ocracoke and adjacent islands is the result of natural selection. Such markings are occasionally found in snakes on the mainland, which means they were already in the genes. Snakes born with this speckling have a better chance of survival, since it helps to camouflage them in the sandy terrain, protecting them from enemies and allowing them to sneak up on their prey. As a result, over the past several thousand years this color pattern has survived and the original mainland coloring has died out.

"They obviously are different, especially on Ocracoke," says Brazwell. He does not agree that the snakes have significant behavioral differences as cited by some scientists, and he affirms that they live not only in the salt marsh but on high sandy ground as well. While he does not identify the snake as a sub-species, he does say that if it were re-described, he could go along with that designation.

All of which leads me to the conclusion that the Outer Banks, Intercapes, or Ocracoke Kingsnake (whichever you choose to call it) is still a mystery. I like it that way. I'm pleased to think that Mother Nature is still able to confound the most knowledgeable of scientists at times, and that life cannot always be captured on a data sheet and displayed on a computer screen. It doesn't surprise me that if something wild and unknowable remains on Earth, it is at Ocracoke.

Shark!

Many people think of sharks when they think of the ocean: big, ferocious sharks of the kind portrayed in the movie Jaws. *For these people the ocean is a place of danger. I seldom think about sharks at all. In all the time I have spent near or on the sea my encounters with them have been few. Once when I was snorkeling off a charter sailboat with a dive team (I was the sailboat's cook) near the Bahamian island of Exuma, I suddenly found myself face to face with a six-foot Hammerhead. We were equally surprised, I think, and after a moment we both made a u-turn and retreated the way we had come.*

Then there was the time my nephew, Bryan Miller, was clamming in the sound near Marsh Haven. The "clam" he brought home was a small sand shark, about three feet long, which he had caught with his rake. I used to snare little sharks in my gill net and, in keeping with my rule of eating whatever I caught, boiled them and flaked off the meat to use in tuna fish casseroles. But I seldom see or think about sharks at Ocracoke, so the big news that had everyone talking in the spring of '97 came as a surprise to me.

It was a warm May afternoon. I was taking Huck for a walk along Firehouse Road (or rather he was taking me) when a blue pickup truck slowed beside me. "Have you seen the shark?" called a man's voice. I shook my head with what must have been a blank expression on my face.

"Shark?" I asked, "What shark?"

The pickup sped up and pulled away, the words, "Go by the fish house," trailing behind it.

As I turned onto Back Road several other people stopped to mention the shark. So I took the short cut across the school yard and onto the main road, heading toward the South Point Fish House on Silver Lake Harbor. I hadn't gotten far before I noticed a stream of slow-moving traffic thicken, coming to a complete halt in front of my destination. A sheriff's deputy was directing traffic. No wonder. The shark was the biggest I had ever seen.

Ten feet, six inches long and weighing 875 pounds, it was a Great White, the second largest ever documented in North Carolina waters. Glen Hopkins, a commercial fisherman from Manteo, had snagged it four miles off the southern tip of Ocracoke. He had caught it by accident while long-lining for smaller species of sharks. It was

enjoying what it must have thought were easy pickings, feeding off the sharks Hopkins and his mate David Caldwell were catching, when it became entangled in the lines. It was already dead when they hauled it up; otherwise, said Hopkins, he would have released it.

Hopkins caused quite a stir when he brought the fish into the South Point Fish House. It was too large to lift off his 46-foot fishing boat, so Nathanial Jackson and his backhoe were employed for the purpose. The traffic backup got so bad as people stopped to look and take pictures that the sheriff's department had to be called.

Big as it was, the shark was not huge by international standards. An immature female, it had yet to reach its adult size, which averages 12 to 15 feet and 1,500 pounds. It was not nearly as big as the star of *Jaws*, but plenty big enough to make you look twice and be glad you were not sharing a swimming pool with it.

Sharks are among the most awe-inspiring, fearsome, and misunderstood creatures on earth. There are more than 300 species currently identified. And while some, such as this Great White, are big and dangerous predators, deserving of their reputation, most are much too small to present any threat to humans, and some are benign plankton-feeders. They are not primitive, slow-witted beasts, as they are often portrayed, but successful, efficient survivors with intelligence that is competitive with rats and birds on behavioral tests.

They belong, along with rays and skates, to the class of fish known as *Chondrichthyes*, or "cartilage fish." Their structure is supported not by bone but by cartilage, which is a flexible, elastic material full of cell spaces. Sharks have a tough, abrasive skin made up of hard, tooth-like scales called denticles. An absence of gill covers and an unspecialized tail fin also help distinguish them from other fish.

Sharks evolved in the Devonian period, about 350 million years ago, and have probably changed little in form since then. Their average size has decreased. The ancestor of the Great White, *Carcharodon*, probably reached a length of 40 to 100 feet, based on fossil teeth that have been identified.

Today sharks range in size from the Dwarf Dogshark, less than seven inches long, to the Whale Shark, which has been reported at more than 60 feet. They are sleek, torpedo-shaped, fast-swimming fish that use their tails as their main source of propulsion. Acute senses, such as keen eyesight and an excellent sense of smell, help them detect and capture prey. Sac-like pores in the head, known as the ampullae of Lorenzini, pick up electrical impulses created by motion.

While some sharks reproduce like fish by dispersing eggs into the water, many species give live birth to their young, and some even have placental-like attachments to their offspring. Shark embryos may feed on their yolks, on other eggs, and some, including the Great White, it is believed, cannibalize their own siblings, eating the smaller, weaker embryos they were born with.

Most sharks have enormous livers which produce vast amounts of oil. This oil helps keep them buoyant, but has also been the reason for excessive hunting in years past, when the oil, which contains vitamin A, was used as a replacement for cod liver oil and for burning in lamps. The oil of some sharks is still used today in making lubricants, skin softeners, lipsticks, and engine de-icers.

The skin of sharks was once used for sandpaper, or shagreen, and is still made into leather. Fertilizer and livestock feed are made from sharks, and large species are hunted for their meat, which is quite tasty. They are also hunted for their fins, which are a high-priced ingredient in Chinese soup (although it is now illegal to "fin" a shark and leave the rest of the body).

White sharks are called *Lamniformes* and are also known as mackerel sharks because of their crescent-shaped tails. They are not actually white, but may range from off-white to grey-brown with white undersides. They have a circulatory modification known as a "rete mirabile" (wonderful net) that allows them to maintain a higher body temperature than the water around them. This gives them extra energy for high-speed chases and attacks. They have large triangular teeth with serrated cutting edges and are, according to one scientist, the "ultimate expression of power and savagery" in the animal world. They are voracious killers, though they prey mostly on fish—and seals, when they can get them. In spite of their reputation, however, white sharks seldom attack humans, and should give swimmers in North Carolina little to fear for they are rare here, particularly large ones.

Exciting as the snagging of the Great White Shark was, of far more economic importance to the area is the Spiny Dogfish. This small shark, less than four feet long, belongs to the order Squaliformes. It is a slow-growing, gray and white shark that can live 25-30 years. Dogfish often travel in large migratory schools, or packs, like dogs, which is where they get their name. They, too, are voracious eaters of all kinds of fish, often getting tangled in nets set for other species and causing problems for commercial fishermen. They show up in North Carolina waters in the winter and are one of the main fisheries at Ocracoke then. They are caught in gill nets and used for fish meal, oil, pet food, and in England as "flake" or "rock salmon" in fish & chips.

Besides the dogfish more than twenty kinds of sharks frequent the coastal waters of the Atlantic, including the Nurse, Bull, Lemon, and Tiger. At Ocracoke, the Mako, Dusky, Black-tip, and Sandbar are caught by long-lining in the ocean during the winter months.

I remember a winter's day a few years ago when a Basking Shark washed up on the beach at Ocracoke. This relatively rare species, which can reach 40 feet in length, is the next largest fish in the world, second only to the whale shark. It is completely harmless, feeding on plankton, which it collects as it swims along with its mouth wide open. A large Basking Shark can filter a metric ton of water per hour as it feeds. It gets its name from its habit of lying, or basking, in the water belly up, a feat made possible by the large quantity of light-weight, buoyant oil in its liver.

Shark fishing has increased dramatically on our Atlantic coast and other areas of the world as other fisheries have declined in recent years. Scientists are concerned that the large species, some of which have been reduced to 25 percent of their former numbers, will disappear. They urge the formation of international treaties to prevent their extinction. Because sharks reproduce late in life and produce only a few offspring, they are slower to rebound than other fish. And while large predatory sharks are not as cute or lovable as some other threatened species, they are just as important in the marine ecosystem. They keep other fish populations healthy by cleaning up their dead and dying, and therefore are imperative for the overall health of our oceans. What's more, their unique white blood cells and resistance to cancer and other diseases may eventually provide answers to human health problems—if they do not disappear from our oceans first.

Sharks make up an important part of the Atlantic fishing economy. They form an essential link, as predators, in the marine food chain. And they represent the sometimes frightening, always fascinating, mystery and danger of the ocean, an allure that both repels and compels us. I hope that the fishing industry and the scientists and legislators who regulate it can reach an agreement that will allow the great sharks of the world to endure. I wouldn't want to come face to face with a Great White like the one I saw at the South Point Fish House. But I like to know that they're out there in the ocean somewhere, fulfilling their ecological role, as they have for millions of years.

Pilgrimage of the black bear

I decided to spend the summer of 1997 working at Ocracoke to save money. With my house rented again, I needed a place to live. I moved to the middle of Silver Lake Harbor and onto Don's sailboat. I sent two of my cats, Scamp and Squirt, to live with "Grandma and Grandpa" in Virginia, and kept Huck and Miss Kelley with me. We traveled to shore and back in kayaks, and Huck perfected his skill at making the three-foot jump off the boat deck and landing correctly in his kayak seat.

Life in the Creek was peaceful. We woke to the sounds of fishermen heading out to check their nets, of clammers getting their gear at Wayne Teeter's Clamhouse, of squabbling laughing gulls and begging mallard ducks. We went ashore to work and to carry on whatever business was needed. It was, for the most part, a pleasant way to spend a summer.

Candy Gaskill was behind the counter of Albert Styron's Store, an old village establishment where Don and I had stopped to get anchor shackles and hot coffee.

"Looks like we've got a little excitement here on Ocracoke today!" she said.

We asked what was going on.

"Andy and Eddie O'Neal saw a bear swim ashore while they were out fishing this morning."

"A bear?" I exclaimed in disbelief.

"Yup." Candy nodded her head solemnly. "Lin Oden even got pictures of it with his polaroid camera. Swam right out of Pamlico Sound, stood up on a sand bar and disappeared into the bushes at Horsepen Point. The National Park Service is looking for it now."

I sat for a moment, coffee cup in hand, absorbing this amazing information. Just the other day I had told my editor at *The Island Breeze* that I was running out of material for my "Sea to Sound" nature column. "I've already written about most of the kinds of animals and plants on the island," I lamented. "Soon there'll be nothing left."

I should have known Mother Nature better than that. She never runs out of surprises. I would never have guessed that my next subject would be an American black bear.

That was 9 a.m on June 17th. By afternoon, the news had spread through the village and was the main topic of conversation. A bear on Ocracoke? No one had ever heard of such a thing. In fact, looking through past records, National Park Service rangers found no evidence that a bear had ever been reported on the island.

The North Carolina Wildlife Commission sent officers to try trap the mysterious visitor. Park rangers posted signs warning campers and hikers to be careful. Rumors ran rampant in the village. The bear was a baby. It was a 500-pound giant. It wasn't a bear at all—it was Bigfoot himself. No, it was a jokester dressed up in a bear skin. Stories circulated that it had been caught and carried away, that it was living in various sections of the village, that its footprints had been observed around some of the restaurant dumpsters.

Another confirmed sighting of the bear came the next day, this time near the Firehouse, and wildlife officers positively identified its footprints. But in spite of all the speculation and searching, the bear was not found. After a few days the search was called off and the warning signs taken down. The notorious visitor was either hiding out (according to Erwin Bauer, author of *Bears in their World*, black bears are "difficult if not impossible to see" in wooded habitat) or it had left the island. ("Maybe it was a day tripper," mused Christine Leslie, referring to the tourists who ride the ferry to Ocracoke for the day and leave before nightfall.) At any rate, *Ursus americanus*, as it is known to scientists, had disappeared.

Where had it come from, anyway, and what was it doing on Ocracoke? Black bears, which roam the forests of most of North America from Canada to Mexico, are plentiful in North Carolina. Hyde County, of which Ocracoke is a part, has one of the highest black bear populations in the state, perhaps in the country. It produces more trophy-size bears than any other area of North Carolina, evidence that the poquosin forests there provide a healthy environment for its ursine residents. They average between 140 and 400 pounds, the bears (males) being considerably larger than the sows (females).

Black bears have a varied diet consisting of nuts, berries, fruits, grasses, small animals, carrion, and occasionally livestock. Their craving for honey and other sweets, made famous by A.A. Milne's *Winnie the Poo*, is real. They forage for their meals over an average home range of 30 to 40 square miles. During mating season—late spring to early summer, the time "our" bear appeared on Ocracoke—males may travel even farther. They are good swimmers. Don and I had watched one swim across Milltail Creek Pond a few years ago from his sailboat, and it seemed quite at ease in the water.

But Pamlico Sound is not Milltail Creek Pond, and Ocracoke Island is not the typical place for a bear to hunt for food or a mate. Nonetheless, this particular bear had indeed swum out of the sound and clambered onto Ocracoke's shore. It may have traveled directly from the mainland, stopping to rest on sand bars along the way. It may have crossed over farther south and island-hopped, working its way up from Cape Lookout and Portsmouth Island.

Once here, it no doubt was exhausted and sought out a cool, hidden spot to sleep. Black bears are normally nocturnal, doing most of their food-seeking at night. It was in the early hours of the morning, around 2 a.m., that the bear was seen wandering in the village. There was concern that it would invade dumpsters, rob campsites, or even kill small pets if it could not get enough of its natural foods to eat. Black bears sometimes appear to have what wildlife author Byron Falrymple describes as a "devil-may-care" vandalism syndrome— an inclination to get into trouble and tear things to pieces. This is especially true if they are hungry.

Our Ocracoke bruin did not cause any trouble, however. Perhaps it was intimidated by the dogs in the village and swam back home. Perhaps it made its way north and crossed the inlet to Hatteras Island. Perhaps it is still here.

Even if we some day learn the fate of our enigmatic bear, we will probably never solve the biggest mystery. Why did it come here in the first place? There were no storms to wash it out to sea, no food shortages or overcrowding to force it out in desperation. What could have possessed it, standing on that distant shore and gazing across that broad expanse of open water, to strike out alone for an unknown

destination, with no maps or charts or safety gear? Could it smell or somehow sense that there was land beyond the waters of the sound? What did it expect to find here? Black bears are credited with being among the most intelligent and inquisitive of animals. Do they also possess qualities, normally associated only with humans, such as a yearning for knowledge, a quest for adventure, a sense of destiny?

I am reminded of the stories of our great epic heroes—some of animals, such as *Watership Down* and *Cold Moons*—others of humans, such as *The Odyssey*. Was our bear following some great mythical quest? Had it embarked upon a pilgrimage to some ursine holy place at Ocracoke, known only to bears? Or was it merely responding to some unknown instinctual or environmental cue which we can not pinpoint?

Scientists have in the past attributed most animal behavior to instinct—an automatic response to physical stimuli. But there is more and more evidence that animals have many of the same emotions and thought patterns that humans have, and that the reasons behind their behaviors are as complex as ours. The black bear's unexpected visit to Ocracoke Island is proof that we do not yet fully understand our fellow inhabitants of Planet Earth.

Barn swallows: nature's most charming pest control

I continued working at the jobs I had begun in the spring. I also cleaned my own cottage, Marsh Haven, hurrying over on Sunday mornings after the renters left and spending as much time as I could, not only dusting and sweeping, but pulling weeds and tending to repairs. Once in a while, if the weather was bad or if some emergency arose, my renters might leave a day or two early. Then I would have my house back for a little while, and I could experience Marsh Haven's summer personality; a part of her I seldom got to see. I might sit on my porch swing with a cold beer, watching the sapphire shades of day as they ripened into rich golds and reds and finally melted into the darkness of night. Just about the time that Venus lit her distant candle above the horizon, the lilting notes of a chuck-will's-widow, or whip-poor-will, as it is locally known, would drift across the marsh from a distant grove of trees, enshrouding Marsh Haven in a spell of magic.

At other times I might sit on the steps and take turns petting the nine formerly wild cats who now considered Marsh Haven their home. If the air was still and there had been a recent rain, I might find myself swatting at a horde of mosquitoes trying to have me for dinner. Even as they feasted on my unprotected arms and legs, a legion of swallows would dart down from their perches on the electric wire and snatch them out of the air in graceful acrobatic maneuvers. Finally, I would hop on my bicycle and pedal back to the harbor, reminding myself that in summer I am only a visitor at Marsh Haven.

I was making sandwiches at the Fig Tree Bakery and Deli when the telephone rang. Another order, I thought, maybe a hummus and veggie on pita bread or a tomato pie with feta cheese, but this call was different. A summer resident, someone I didn't know, had gotten my name from the National Park Service.

"I'm sorry to bother you," the woman said, "but we have a problem and we don't know what to do. There is a swallow's nest on our front porch, and four or five of the babies have fallen out and are dead or dying!"

Ocracoke is home to lots of barn swallows in the summertime. They flit through the air in graceful maneuvers, feeding on the abundant mosquitoes and other flying insects, and build mud nests in the eaves of homes, restaurants, and other buildings. They sit in rows on telephone wires, their distinctive forked tails making them easy to identify, chirping with one another about swallow business. You can hear them at dawn, twittering in a liquid cacophony of musical tones.

I tried to get more details from the caller. How old were the birds? Were they hatchlings? Nestlings? Fledglings? Were they feathered yet? Had the nest collapsed? Were the parents around? Were they trying to feed the dethroned youngsters?

As a wildlife rehabilitator, I am trained to respond to situations such as this. But this summer I was living on a sailboat, and most of my rehabilitator's books and equipment were packed away. What's more, there was no room to house birds on the boat, which I was sharing with a cat, a large dog, and another person. Swallow nest-lings are more difficult to raise than most other birds, due to their requirements for a highly specialized diet. The best solution to the problem, I knew, would be to put them back where they came from, if that was possible.

"I'll come over as soon as I get off work," I said, "but in the meantime do you think you can get them back in the nest?" The woman said she would try.

When I got off work at 7:30 that evening, I followed the direc-tions the woman had given me to a house overlooking one of the branches of Oyster Creek. Several swallows swooped and darted as the owners met me on the deck.

"Floss and Rich Sobel," they introduced themselves. "We couldn't reach to get them back in the nest. We've been trying to borrow a taller ladder but haven't been able to locate one so far. Here are the babies."

Several tiny, bedraggled brown forms filled a small container.

"One was dead, and I buried it," Rich said. "But these four are still alive. There is the nest they fell out of."

He pointed to a light fixture above his head.

As I watched, a swift form flitted across the porch and hovered close to the nest.

"Yes!" I cried in excitement. "That must be one of the parents. Let me take a look at the nest and maybe we can get them back in."

With Rich's assistance I was able to balance on the top rung of the step ladder and peer over the light fixture. On top was a nest fastened with hardened mud, a typical barn swallow's nest. A lone nestling gawked at me. I breathed a quick prayer that my interference would not cause the parents to desert the nest and cost this little fellow his life.

"Please hand me the babies, one by one," I asked Floss and Rich.

As they did, I slid the frail bodies into the shallow nest as gently as I could, making sure I did not disturb the one still up there. I was afraid they would tumble out again, too weak to hold on, but they clung to home with what seemed to be relief and happiness.

Now for the real test. Would the parents come back and accept the cast-offs? Would they feed them again? Let them stay in the nest? The answers lay in whatever caused the babies to have fallen or be pushed out. They were obviously too young to have fledged and left the nest for natural reasons.

Sometimes if the babies are sick or deformed, the parents will push them out to give the healthy offspring a better chance, I explained as we waited. Perhaps they had unknowingly fed the babies insects which had been sprayed with pesticides, causing them to sicken. Perhaps they had themselves ingested pesticides before the eggs were laid, leading to mutations and deformities in the young.

I had read that severe food shortage caused high mortality among nestlings. Swallows feed strictly on flying insects, and this had been a dry summer with low populations of mosquitoes. Maybe the babies were starving and the parents had pushed them out, knowing they could not feed them. On the other hand, maybe something had simply caused them to fall, and once reinstated, everything would be fine. Floss, Rich, and I hoped that this was the case.

We didn't have to wait long. One of the adult swallows approached the nest, darting back and forth. After a moment it stopped, and we could see that it was feeding a baby. The other parent soon followed, and there was no indication that they were trying to displace the reinstated nestlings. We watched for a while, but the family appeared to be functioning normally. By now it was growing dark, so I asked Rich and Floss to keep me posted, climbed into my pickup truck, and headed back to the village. I paddled my kayak back out to the boat where I was living and called it a night.

Barn, or common, swallows are members of the family Hirundinidae, along with purple martins and cliff, tree, bank, and rough-winged swallows. Their scientific name, *Hirundo rustica*, means "swallow of the country," and they are indeed the member seen most often throughout the countryside. They are slim, sparrow-sized birds with long pointed wings, forked tails, and short beaks. Their upperside is glossy blue-black, with a creamy underside and rust throat. Excellent eyesight helps them catch the tiny flying insects they feed on. They spend almost all of their time in the air, and consequently are excellent fliers; it is estimated that they may travel 600 miles per day as they pursue their tiny prey. They have small weak legs, however, which make them clumsy on the ground.

The swallows arrive in Ocracoke in late spring after a long journey north from South America, during which they travel by day and rest by night. After mating, the male and female build a nest, or rebuild a former nest, using mud, grass and feathers as a lining. The female lays four to six brown-spotted white eggs (the nest on the Sobels' porch had six), which hatch in approximately two weeks. The hatchlings are altricial, which means they are born featherless and completely dependent on their parents. They are ready to fledge, or leave the nest, in about three weeks, but hang around with Mom and Pop for a few days before setting out on their own. The adults often raise a second family before the season is over, and the fledglings sometimes help feed their younger siblings.

Ocracokers welcome the barn swallows, as well as their cousins the purple martins, for not only are they lovely and entertaining, they do an excellent job of helping to reduce the mosquito population. They seem to enjoy human proximity and often build their nests in the eaves of houses. They are among the most charming mosquito control agents available.

A message from Floss awaited me when I arrived at the Fig Tree the next morning. "All's well", it said.

That evening, however, she called back. One of the babies had tumbled out again, and Rich had put it back. This happened several times over the next few days, and Rich buried two more nestlings before the remaining three finally reached the age of fledging. When I last stopped by, the surviving babies were unrecognizable, looking just like the parents, but they were still hanging around the light fixture. The nest itself, however, was gone. Floss and Rich had found the pieces of it lying on the porch deck a day or so before.

I wondered, as I thought back upon the little ongoing drama, if the nest, which the Sobels said had been used each summer for about six years, had finally filled up and become too shallow to contain the growing babies, or if parasites had made it uninhabitable. Perhaps the parents had purposely torn it down when their offspring were old enough to leave. I wonder if they will build a new nest there next year, or search out a different site. I look forward to the continuing story of the Sobels' barn swallow family.

Cicadas:
summer music makers

Summer was not my favorite time on Ocracoke; it was too hot, humid, and above all crowded, particularly in the village. With all my jobs (earning money was, after all, the reason I had decided to stay) I seemed to do little besides work. Still, there were pleasant times; evenings spent chatting with friends at the Tiki, an outdoor bar; nights relaxing on the boat and listening to the music of Martin Garrish and Jim Wynn as it floated across the water from the Jolly Roger.

And an occasional exciting experience kept life interesting. A sudden thunderstorm struck terror in the Creek. I was on shore with Huck when I saw it coming, so I hurried him into the kayak and we raced out to the boat. I paddled furiously against a strong wind that was already painting whitecaps on the harbor and glanced nervously at the bolts of lightning that were cracking the darkened sky. Once on Aurora, I shoved Huck and Miss Kelley into the cabin, closed the hatch, and began securing the boat as best I could. But the wind had turned into a howling monster, and I could barely stand. Lashing rain had reduced visibility to nearly zero when suddenly, only a few yards away, I saw the ghost-like shape of a huge boat, twice as heavy as Aurora, bearing down on us with all the fury that Mother Nature could muster.

I started to fight my way to the bow to fend her off; then realizing the hopelessness of that, I hurried back to Huck and Miss Kelley. Clutching them in my arms, I huddled in the cockpit and listened for the crack of splintering wood. When it didn't come, I crept back up and peered into the storm. The boat was only an arm's reach away now, but its calamitous rush toward us had ended.

At the last moment, its captain had managed to start his engine and gain control of his run-away craft, torn loose from its anchorage by the storm. Others were not so lucky; several collisions occurred as Mother Nature played pick-up-sticks with the boats in the harbor. But Aurora and her crew were unharmed, and I returned to work as usual the next day.

"What is that awful noise?"

A tourist lady, well dressed in a trim pants suit, was addressing me. I was behind the antique bakery case at the Fig Tree waiting for her to select whatever might strike her fancy. I looked askance and cocked my ear when she repeated her question. Someone had been putting a new roof on the building next door, and on another lot some-one was cutting down cedar trees, so I listened for the screech of saws, chain or circular. I heard neither, so I looked at her puzzled.

"That noise!" she repeated with agitation. "It kept my husband awake last night and it's been driving us crazy ever since we arrived."

As she spoke she gestured in a vague all-encompassing manner out beyond the screen door, and it suddenly occurred to me what she meant.

"You mean that kind of buzzing sound?"

She nodded.

"They're cicadas," I said, but the look on her face told me that she had no idea what I was talking about. "They're a kind of insect. They're in the trees."

The lady shuddered as her expression turned to disgust.

"They're not bad," I said defensively, "They're harmless, fascinating insects. I like them. I love to listen to them."

She made her purchase and left thinking, I'm sure, that I was as strange as the noise that annoyed her.

I was amazed that anyone could find the sound of the cicadas disturbing. Many a day I sit on my porch swing sipping a cup of coffee or glass of wine, choosing to leave the stereo off so I can enjoy the symphony of music produced by the insects and frogs that live around my house. On warm days in late summer and fall Ocracoke is filled with the resonance of cicada song, a continuous buzz that begins at a low timbre, rises in cadence, and subsides again.

Sometimes fallaciously known as locusts, to which they have no resemblance, cicadas are large insects of the family *Cicadidae*. They belong, along with aphids and leafhoppers, to the order *Homoptera* (the true "bugs"). Cicadas live in various areas of the earth, and more than 75 species reside in the eastern United States. Each has its own distinct life cycle, variation of song, and time of day for singing.

Like other insects, members of the family *Cicadadae* are invertebrates wearing their protective skeleton, which is made of chitin, on the outside of their bodies. They have a head, thorax, and abdomen with three pairs of legs attached to the thorax. They grow to adulthood by proceeding though stages, known as metamorphosis.

Cicadas spend most of their lives underground, using enlarged, shovel-like forelegs to tunnel through the ground and pointed beaks to suck sap from tree roots. In this wingless nymphal state they go through a series of molts, each time exchanging their exoskeleton for a larger size. The first stage, after emerging from the egg, is described by Edwin Way Teale as resembling a "tiny finless fish." The well-known 17-year locust (cicada) may molt 30 times in the 17 years it spends below the ground, but other species have shorter life cycles.

Depending on the species, cicadas spend from two to 20 years underground, finally digging out of their tunnels, emerging into daylight, and climbing up a nearby tree or other solid object. The back of the exoskeleton splits open, and in this final molt the mature winged cicada forces its way out. It flies to a protected spot in a tree where it can feed on the sap of twigs for the remaining days or weeks of its life.

The cicada is one of the heaviest insects in relation to its wing size, making flight a real accomplishment. It has two sets of membranous wings which, like other members of the Homoptera order, it folds like a peaked roof when not in flight.

The droning song for which cicadas are so well known is made by the males as they court their ladies. It is claimed to be the loudest sound produced in the insect kingdom, made with a pair of shell-like drums and a complex series of resonators located on the base of the thorax. When the drums are vibrated the resulting sounds are modified by the resonators.

Tympanic organs, or *chordatonae*, enable cicadas to hear one another. These hearing organs, thin membranes which are similar to our eardrums, are located on both sides of the base of the abdomen. They vibrate when sound waves strike them, transmitting sound waves to the insect's brain. The singing of one male may inspire nearby cicadas to join in, creating a symphony which rises and falls in harmony. Females distinguish members of their own species by their songs and choose mates accordingly.

After they mate, female cicadas make slits in tree twigs where they lay their eggs. They die shortly thereafter. When the eggs hatch the tiny emerging nymphs fall to the ground and tunnel down to the dark, subterranean world where they will spend most of their lives.

Enemies of cicadas include a fungus of the genus *Cordyceps*, which attack cicada nymphs underground and, when mature, sends up a bright red or orange fruiting body that may rise two to three inches above ground; strange apparitions known as "flowering cicadas." In some areas of the world, cicadas are eaten regularly by humans.

By far the most aggressive and highly adapted pursuer of cicadas, however, is the cicada-killer wasp. It is said that you can hear the death-cry of a cicada when it is speared by the stinger of this largest of American wasps. It is not actually killed, however, but paralyzed. The wasp transports the immobile cicada, much heavier than itself, into a burrow prepared for the purpose. There she lays a single egg within its body. The egg hatches into a larva, and the larva feeds on the cicada until it is mature and ready to molt into an adult wasp and fly free. It is a ghoulish but fascinating tale, one of the many dramas taking place around us as we dwell, unaware, on this earth. Summers at Ocracoke are punctuated not only by the sonorous buzzing of cicada mating calls but also by the appearance, in often unexpected places, of their rejected nymphal exoskeletons. I found one clinging to the nozzle of my outdoor shower and another attached to my porch railing. I rather enjoyed the slightly macabre new decor, so I left them until nature removed them with a strong wind. If you look closely at the ground where you find a shed skin and you may spot the hole dug by the emerging cicada nymph.

The ancient Greeks told a story about a cicada that helped win a music contest, thus making it the symbol for melody. Nature writer Laura C. Martin writes that the Cherokee know it as the "jarfly," and that the saying "the jarfly has brought the beans" refers to the fact that cicadas begin to sing in mid-summer when the beans are beginning to ripen. The peasants in nineteenth century France believed, according to philosopher/scientist J. Henri Fabre, that "at harvest-time, the Cicada sings, "Sego, sego, sego! Reap, reap, reap!" to encourage them to work." Indeed, one of the nicknames given to the cicada is the "harvest-fly."

For myself, the peaceful drone of cicadas tends to cajole me not into a frenzy of work but into a pleasant state of laziness. I agree with the French philosopher Jean-Paul Sartre, who says that while cicadas may accomplish a mating requirement with their songs, they also are "expressing the joy of living, the universal joy which every animal species celebrates after its kind."

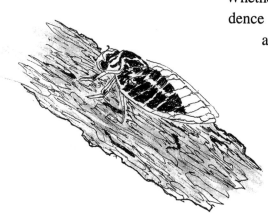

Whether you perceive their cadence as an "awful noise," or as "music to one's ears," cicadas are a memorable part of hot southern summer afternoons, of lazy and idyllic times spent on the Outer Banks.

Winged enigmas:
Ocracoke's bats

I was glad that summer was coming to an end. Already the number of tourists had declined, and soon I would be able to move back into my house. I would miss living in the middle of the harbor on Aurora and traveling to and from the village by kayak. Not including, that is, the time Huck and I flipped over in the middle of the harbor, losing all the gear and having a horrendous struggle getting dog, kayak, paddle, and myself back to the sailboat. That was before Huck learned to swim, and rescuing him was the biggest challenge of all.

I couldn't wait to putter around in my garden, gather all my cats back together, and sink into a hot bath in my clawfoot tub. It would also be nice to have my word processor back. I still had a few weeks to go, though. I took advantage of the time by going to the beach, kayaking in the sound, and wandering around the village.

It was September 8th, the tail-wagging end of a mild Ocracoke summer, when I saw at last what I had been looking for all season.

I had gotten off work an hour earlier and had ridden my bicycle to the Lifeguard Beach to ponder the thundering waves whipped up by Hurricane Erika as she moved up the coast. I was grateful that she had plotted her course far to the east, leaving our weather balmy and still with only the rowdy surf betraying her distant presence.

Later, I picked up Huck and was walking to the harbor beneath the canopy of trees that line both sides of the Back Road. Twilight, that ambiguous time of day when shadows merge quietly into the ebony darkness of encroaching night, was descending on the village.

Suddenly, a small, dark shape darted down in front of us, its sharp lines silhouetted against the sky. Huck and I spotted it at the same time, his ears going up as he followed its erratic flight, my eyes alighting as I exclaimed softly to myself: "Yes! At last!"

There before us, voraciously pursuing mosquitoes, was a small flying mammal—a bat. We watched its acrobatic performance of dives and twirls for several moments before it disappeared into the labyrinth of darkening branches and sky. I searched for another as we completed our walk home, but saw no more.

I had been interested in the presence (or absence) of bats at Ocracoke for several years. I was always asking friends, "Have you seen any bats this year?" or "Did you used to see bats here?" I was sure that I remembered watching their antics in the mid-'80s, but had seen very few in recent years. The abundance of mosquitoes and other flying insects would seem to provide excellent feeding ground for bats, although I wasn't sure where they would roost.

When Ann Lochery came to me with the idea of introducing bat houses on the island as a means of promoting non-toxic mosquito control, I determined to follow through with my interest and learn more about Ocracoke's winged mammals. What species were, or had been, here? Did they live on the island or just migrate through? Where did they roost? Had they declined in numbers? If so why, and what could be done about it? Learning the answers proved to be no easy task.

Bats, which make up the order *Chiroptera*, are the only mammals capable of true flight. Their forelimbs are adapted to form wings, with thin membranes stretched across long, delicate fingers back to the ankle of the hind legs. Another membrane extends between the hind legs. To capture insects, they scoop them into their tail or wing membranes, then reach down with their heads and flick them into their mouths. Such adaptations make them excellent and agile fliers but they are severely limited in any other kind of locomotion.

They spend their days (and in some species their winters) folded up and hanging by their claws in protected areas such as caves, attics, tree cavities, or tree foliage. They are almost completely nocturnal. While their eyesight is not bad (blind as a bat is a misleading saying,) they use a sophisticated echo-location system that enables them to navigate and hunt insects in the dark. They emit ultrasonic sounds through their mouth and nose and receive echoes through their ears in a method much like modern sonar.

Because insects, the primary food of most species of Chiroptera, are not available in the winter in temperate climates, these bats either migrate south for the winter or hibernate. They normally breed in the fall and females store the sperm until spring, at which time their eggs are fertilized. In colonial species the females separate from the males at this time and form nursery colonies where they bear one or two hairless or nearly hairless, blind young in late spring. The pups are able to fly by the end of summer, and to breed by fall. The average life span of most temperate bat species is 10 to 15 years, and some have been known to live more than 20.

Throughout history bats have been a source of mystery and often fear (as illustrated by their association with Halloween), but they are actually gentle, interesting animals whose insect-eating and flower-pollinating habits make them extremely beneficial to humans. A single bat can eat more than one half of its body weight in a night— 3,000 insects. They save farmers billions of dollars each year by consuming crop pests, and it has been estimated that they are responsible for up to 98% of rain forest regrowth in cleared areas in Latin America.

Bats are among the mammals known to contract rabies, but fewer than one percent carry it. Few people in this country have contracted rabies from bats, but it is unwise to touch one or pick it up.

Bats occur throughout the world except in the polar regions, and are second only to rodents in number of species. Today, however, they are among our most endangered animals, due primarily to loss of roosting areas, but also due to extermination by people who do not understand them or appreciate their value. While some kinds of bats eat fruits and nectars and a few (the notorious vampires, for example) drink blood, North Carolina's 15 bat species are all insectivores.

Dr. Thomas L. Quay of North Carolina State University, in his three-year-long cataloguing of animals on the Outer Banks in the late 1950s, listed only one species of Chiroptera on the Banks; the Red Bat. A recent update, *Birds and Mammals of the Cape Hatteras National Seashore: Thirty-five Years of Change*, by James Parnell and William David Webster, added two species: the Evening Bat, recorded in different areas of Dare County, and the Silver-Haired Bat, recorded in Ocracoke. This update again included the Red Bat, commenting that it was locally abundant on Hatteras Island during fall and spring migrations, but was not observed at Ocracoke. These records, however, are probably far from complete.

Ten to 12 species of bats are found on North Carolina's coastal plain, according to Mary Kay Clark of the N.C. Museum of Natural History. It is likely that several of these pass through the barrier islands, even though they have not been recorded. It is probable too that all three species mentioned in the studies can be found at Ocracoke, even though only one was actually spotted.

Do these bats mate and raise their young here, or just pass through in migration? No data seems to exist on this. The Outer Banks islands probably do not provide adequate roosting sites for colonial species. But such solitary species as the Red and Silver-haired bats, which roost singly in the foliage of trees, might indeed produce young on the islands. Besides roosting in trees, they find shelter in the eaves and attics of old buildings, and one long-time Ocracoke resident said he remembers bats roosting on the electric poles that run the length of the island.

Has the bat population at Ocracoke declined in recent years? I received mixed responses to this question as I questioned island locals. Clinton Gaskill, who has lived here most of his 91 years, says he does not remember a lot of bats in his youth, but there were some of what he called "level-winged bats" in the village. According to some old-timers Ocracoke definitely had more bats in earlier times, particularly in the '40s. Lawton Howard, on the other hand, says there never were a lot of bats at Ocracoke. Whatever the case, the limiting factor seems not to be food, for there are plenty of flying insects, but roosting habitat.

Does it make sense to put up bat houses? "Sure," says Mary Kay Clark. In fact, she said, that would be an excellent way to find the answers to many of the questions I was asking. She recommended working in conjunction with an organization called Bat Conservation International in their North American Bat House Research Project.

They could not only provide us with useful information for setting up houses; we could contribute to their knowledge of Chiroptera's natural history and conservation on the Outer Banks.

So I still do not really know what kind of bat I saw on the evening of September 8th. I don't know where it came from or where it was going, or if perhaps it would like to stop and make Ocracoke its home. But I hope that before too long we can answer some of these questions, and if bats do indeed have a place in Ocracoke's natural ecosystem, that we can give them a helping hand, provide them with free housing and enlist their help in controlling insect pests. I would much prefer to stroll outside on a summer evening and watch bats flitting about than swat blood-thirsty mosquitoes.

Autumn sojourners:
Monarch butterflies

Each season, each year, I seem to find some new cause for amazement on Ocracoke. It is as if Mother Nature fears that I will be overwhelmed if she reveals herself all at once; so she surprises me with unexpected gifts. It is not always a matter of happening upon some new phenomenon; it is more often a different way of looking at something I have seen countless times before; of opening my eyes and my heart at precisely the same moment so that some ordinary subject is illuminated and I can see its real magic. While the moment may not last, the sense of wonder does.

I was on my way home from Richmond, returning from my monthly visit with family and friends. As usual, I had hated telling them goodbye but was now anxious to get home. I was exhausted, not only by the six-hour drive but also by the many errands I always had to do, tasks that could not easily be accomplished on an isolated island. As my truck lumbered across the ramp from the ferry onto home territory, my only thought was to get back to Marsh Haven, unpack, and relax. Soon, however, I forgot all about my weariness.

Bright-colored, fairy-like shapes fluttered around me as I drove down Ocracoke's Highway 12 on a late October afternoon. Heading back to the village from the ferry terminal at the north end of the island, I noticed the fragrance of fall in the air.

Above me the sky was a soft robin's egg blue. On my left, russet-colored sea oats lined the dunes, waving briskly in the breeze. Golden-hued spartina grass made a sharp contrast to the pewter tones of needlerush on my right, where the salt marsh melded into Pamlico Sound. And on both sides, moving in the same southerly direction as I, flitted the lovely orange and black forms of monarch butterflies.

I was caught between jubilant wonder and fearful apprehension as I hurtled past them in my 1986 Dodge pickup. Beside me, Huck solemnly watched the road and perked up his ears when one of the ephemeral shapes soared in front of us.

"Hurtled" is a relative term, since I had actually slowed to 40 mph to avoid hitting any of the butterflies, but compared to their haphazard fluttering it seemed like an unholy and devastating speed. Usually the updraft created by moving vehicles would push the butterflies out of the way, but the broken, sadly waving orange wings that lined the sides of the highway were proof that many had fallen victim to human travelers. I didn't want to add to that toll.

I was in the midst of one of Mother Nature's great annual events; the autumnal migration of the monarch butterflies. All across the United States these lovely familiar insects were on the move. Highway 12 formed one of the eastern-most land corridors for their long journey south to Mexico, where the four-inch-winged travelers would gather by the millions to spend the winter.

Slow and erratic as their flight seemed to be, it would carry them hundreds, even thousands, of miles to their winter homes and, if entomologists are right, back again in the spring. Indeed, many of the colorful monarchs around me had no doubt already traversed a great distance, coming from Canada, New England, and other areas to the north. While not as famous as the monarchs of Pacific Grove, California, these butterflies were embarked on an equally fantastic journey.

Their route had probably taken them down the Eastern Shore of Virginia, across the Chesapeake Bay, and along Nags Head and Hatteras Islands to the north. Seaside goldenrod, which forms a brilliant curtain of yellow along many of Ocracoke's roadsides, would provide sustenance to strengthen them for the rest of their journey. Much of the trip would be, and had already been, across water where no food was available, so they were dependent on the prolific goldenrod which bloomed along the coast in fall.

Danaus plexippus, as the monarch is known to entomologists, belongs to the subfamily *Daninae*, the milkweed butterflies. Like other insects, they have a head, a thorax, an abdomen, and six legs. Along with most butterflies they have two pairs of scale-covered wings, a tube-like proboscis, long clubbed antennae containing sensory organs; and fly during the day. Being cold-blooded, they depend on outside sources to provide their body heat. This is why they are often seen basking in the sun. Butterflies pass through four stages in their lives: the egg, the larva (or caterpillar,) the pupa (or chrysalis,) and the adult butterfly.

The milkweed butterflies are so known because in their larval stage they feed entirely on milkweed, a bitter, poisonous plant. Adult monarch butterflies continue to eat and store the noxious cardiac glycosides found in the milkweed, making them distasteful to would-be predators. This mechanism protects not only them, but also the tasty viceroy butterflies which emulate monarch color patterns and fool their predators.

Once the migrating butterflies reached their destination in Mexico they would spend about five months clinging together to branches of trees, dormant. They would become active again in early spring and mate. Only about one percent would survive to return, but these, mostly females, would retrace their route to their North American homes. Sometime around May or June they would lay single eggs on the underside of milkweed leaves. Then, their journey over, they would die.

After a week the eggs would hatch into smooth, ringed black, green and yellow caterpillars, which would feed exclusively on milkweed leaves. After molting about five times they would spin a bright green chrysalis, or pupa, continue their development, and finally emerge from the chrysalis as butterflies.

While there are three species of milkweed butterflies (*Danainae*) in the United States, the monarch is the only one known to undertake long migrations. Scientists believe that their antennae may have some magnetic sense that guides them. Many questions are unanswered, however, and the details of their unique life histories are not fully understood. Tagging projects, which use acrylic glue to attach plastic numbered tags to the undersides of monarch wings, attempt to determine their routes and habits.

The Outer Banks are known for their beautiful beaches, their wonderful fishing, their myriad species of water birds. They are renowned as part of the migration path for shore birds, song birds, and even "snow birds," those human travelers who move south in the fall via sailboat, motor home, or any other way they can propel themselves to warm climates. The migration routes of dolphins and whales, sea turtles and eels all lie close to the shores of our islands. But none is more astounding than the phenomenal journey of the fragile, fairy-like monarch butterflies, often unnoticed and seldom celebrated as they pass silently but ceaselessly along these slender strands of sand and salt marsh.

Ocracoke's most common wild animals: cats

Ocracoke, like many islands, is a cat place. Almost every household has at least one (usually more) contented, fastidious feline perched on the front porch or peering out a window. It is one of the many things I love about the island. All the cats here do not, however, have happy homes. Some can be seen haunting the garbage dumpsters, hiding in the woods, darting across the road along the National Seashore. Known as feral cats, they are wild and homeless. For them life is a constant struggle against disease, starvation, automobiles, and roaming dogs. They seldom live long, but the damage they do to songbird populations is devastating. As a wildlife rehabilitator I know first hand how many birds are killed or injured by cats.

I became interested in Ocracoke's cats as soon as I moved here. I gave a hand, now and then, to Margaret Harris, a woman who started an organization called Ocracats, whose mission was to spay and neuter the feral cats. When she decided to move to Maine, she asked me to take over.

"No way!" I responded. "Wildlife rehabilitation is the only unpaid job I can afford."

I did agree, however, to handle the small fund she had accumu-

lated in case there was a cat emergency. I held out for about three months, but somehow, without intending to do it, I found myself starting Ocracats up again. The program operates entirely on money donated by concerned cat lovers. Its primary goal is to "neuter and release" feral cats of both sexes. It also pays the veterinary bills for feral cats that are injured or become ill.

Seldom a day goes by that I do not receive a call about some cat on the island. I loan out cages, help in trapping, and assist Jane Rowley, Ocracoke's part-time veterinarian, with them. I also try and find them homes when possible.

The National Park Service truck pulled up outside my house and Allan Buss, a seasonal ranger, climbed out. He had called a few minutes earlier. He wore a concerned expression as he greeted me and opened the back door of the vehicle.

"A tourist found it up near the campground, on the Nature Trail. It's really bad," he warned me. "I've never seen anything so pitiful."

Reaching behind the seat, he lifted out a mottled brown bundle of fur and bones. "It must have been somebody's pet once. It's not wild."

It was a cat, an adult female. It had long tabby-colored fur and no doubt had once been a beautiful animal. Now reduced to a skeleton, its fur was matted and missing in patches, its eyes running with the symptoms of a respiratory illness.

Allan was right. It was pitiful. As I took it in my arms I found it hard to believe that an animal so thin could still be alive. Allan told me that he had offered it some food but it had only eaten a few bites. He had called me because someone had told him I worked with the unwanted, feral cats on the island. I assured him that I would do whatever I could, but I was not overly optimistic.

After Allan left I put the cat, whom I nicknamed "Myrtle," in a cage I had prepared for it. It was very gentle and did not try to escape. I offered it some food, but it showed no interest. I was out of antibiotics, so I called Ruth Fordon, a friend who also works with cats on the island. She brought over some Clavamox and we gave it a first dose.

I was concerned that the cat was suffering from either of two communicable, deadly diseases prevalent on the island. I had it tested for feline leukemia and feline immune deficiency virus (FIV), the cat equivalent of human AIDS, and was relieved when both tests came back negative. At least the cat would have a chance.

Ocracoke and other Outer Banks islands are full, however, of cats that have no such chance. They are domestic cats that by accident or intent have been forced to go wild. These feral cats proliferate and have a major impact on the island ecosystem. They are the most commonly seen "wild" animals here.

The cats of Ocracoke have a colorful history, as legend has it. According to local lore, they first came over with the early settlers in the 1700s, some perhaps with the pirates. They were kept on ships to keep down rat populations, and at Ocracoke they had the same task.

The problem is that cats multiply faster than needed for rat control. They live in areas far from the villages, where rats are not a problem anyway. And it isn't only rats that they kill to survive, but all kinds of birds and other wild creatures.

The day after Allan brought the sick cat, I looked out my window to see one of the feral cats that lives near me chasing something. As

I hurried through the door I saw that it was a green snake, an attractive, harmless reptile seen less and less often at Ocracoke. Before I could rescue it the cat snatched it and ran into the woods.

Two days later a female cardinal was brought to me. It had been rescued from the jaws of a cat, but was too badly injured to survive. One may be tempted to justify these actions by saying that it is "Nature's way." But the fact is, domestic cats are NOT part of nature. They have been domesticated for thousands of years, and have no counterparts in the wild. They did not evolve as part of the Outer Banks wildlife, and can only bring harm to a an ecosystem that is already fragile and at risk.

The birds and other wildlife are not the only ones that suffer. A life in the wild is terribly hard on the cats themselves. Studies show that while cats raised in human homes live an average of 10 to 15 years, the average life span of a feral cat is two to three years. These years are spent, for the most part, scared, hungry, and often sick.

The two illnesses mentioned earlier, feline leukemia and feline AIDS, run rampant through some feral cat colonies. They are slow killers which cause much suffering, often killing off whole litters of kittens before they reach adulthood. There are other communicable diseases that also strike hard at feral cats. While they do help to keep cat populations under control, they do so in a cruel, painful way.

Myrtle, the cat brought to me, was not a typical feral cat. She was gentle and tame, and had obviously once had a home. How did she come to be wandering, starved and sick, in the woods far from the village? We wondered if she had been lost, or perhaps was dropped off by some well-meaning person who no longer wanted her and thought she would fare well as a wild cat. It happens again and again. But she was lucky; she was rescued by Allan.

All feral cat stories do not have such happy endings. Recently I found a cat lying in the road, just hit by a car. It had been eating something it had found on the pavement. I held it in my arms, seeking a heartbeat that wasn't there, giving it the only human affection it may have ever known. There was nothing else I could do.

Another time I received a phone call about a sick cat. It was a big black male that had been hanging around a neighborhood for more than a year, raiding garbage cans and stealing the food put out for tame cats. He would not let anyone touch him, I was told; but now, emaciated and ill, he was easy to pick up, put into a cage, and carry to the veterinarian. He tested negative for feline leukemia and diabetes, but the last test result was bad news. He was suffering from feline AIDS, and there was no cure.

I didn't have him put to sleep right away, however, for sick though he was, he had become the happiest cat imaginable. Having never had human care or kindness, he now lapped it up like warm milk. I put him in a large crate away from my other cats, gave him kitty litter and a box with a blanket, and I fed him lots of good canned cat food. You would have thought he had a suite at the Hilton. He never tried to get out, and he purred with pure pleasure whenever I spoke to him or stroked him. The antibiotics we put him on lessened his symptoms temporarily, and I spoiled him rotten for a couple weeks. When he became worse I took him back to the vet and as I petted him, she put him to sleep. Even at the end he was purring with happiness.

Ocracoke is full of cat lovers, people who do everything they can to help alleviate the suffering of the feral cats. They spend their own money and time feeding and trying to find homes for these unwanted cats. The only long-term solution, however, is to reduce the number of "wild" cats running free on the island. Only by neutering and, when possible, keeping cats indoors, can we help Ocracoke's cats and wildlife stay alive and healthy. There will always be enough cats to keep down the rat population; let us hope that there will not be so many that they destroy the wildlife populations and suffer a cruel, loveless life as well.

Myrtle's story had a surprise ending. She regained her appetite and her respiratory infection cleared up. She remained thin, however, so I took her to a veterinarian in Richmond where she was diagnosed as having hyperthyroidism. She was placed on medication and, when it ran out, I took her to a veterinarian who was on the island for the day. When I removed her from the cage Trish Palmisano, an Ocracoker who was in the room, immediately cried out "Critter!"

Myrtle was her cat and before disappearing she had been on treatment for her illness. She was not one to roam, so how she got all the way to the campground, miles away, was a mystery. Perhaps some well-meaning tourist, thinking she had no home, picked her up and lost her there. She was finally returned to her real owner, a loving human who would take care of her. The rest of Ocracoke's cats deserve as much.

Circles in the sand

One day Tony McGowan, the owner of the newspaper for which I write, came by to drop off film. I gave him a tour of Marsh Haven, and a sailor at heart, he exclaimed, "I could live here! It's just like being on a boat." I knew what he meant. My little cottage has the feeling of being as much outdoors as indoors, just like a sailboat. Early February of 1998 almost turned Marsh Haven into a boat, or at least the semblance of one. Looking out the window, I found my-self completely surrounded by a sea of undulating water!

The wind had been blowing relentlessly from the west for days. It was the topic of conversation wherever you went. "When will it stop?" islanders asked each other, complaining that it was making them too restless to relax or to work. The water at the little soundside beach where I take Huck was pushed up against the marsh grass, leaving no place to walk. The sound had no low tides; the shallows stayed deep and tipped with whitecaps all day long. The water in the creek beside my house rose higher every day, and the cries of gulls and fish crows, fighting to stay airborne and on course, echoed constantly. Then one cloudless day an unusually high tide and a particularly strong wind, not content with the havoc they had already wrought, teamed up and pushed the sound right over its banks and into the marshes and yards that bordered it.

As the water rose, I hurried to move my truck, parking it on the ramp that led into my neighbor's garage. I tied my kayak to a tree and packed ladder, shovel, etc. under the house so they would not float away. All along the sound side of the island people were similarly engaged as they watched the water rise. Before long my lawn was submerged. I saw the boardwalk I had recently built lift up and float across the yard. I worried about the outside cats, but the deck where they stayed was tall enough to be safe. Putting on my high rubber boots, I tried to walk to the village, but the water in the road was soon above my knees, so I gave up. I watched as first one porch step, then another, disappeared from view. Fortunately, the water did not reach the first floor, but it remained high for several days. Then the wind "came around" to the east and died down. It took days to clean up the mess and repair the damage, but Ocracoke finally returned to normal.

"Hey, Don, come over here, I think we've been visited by aliens," I called across the hundred or so feet of ocean beach that separated us. I ignored his look of derision.

"Seriously, there were flying saucers here, I'm sure. Look at all the signs they left. Signals, no doubt, to someone up in outer space."

It was early February, and Don and I were walking along the dune line at the beach, not far from the Pony Pens. An errant storm had passed through a few days before, pounding the shore with wind and waves and scattering the beach with whelk shells and scotch bonnets. At my insistence Don reluctantly strolled over to the edge of the dune where I was standing and looked down at the sand where I pointed. A perfectly symmetrical configuration of concentric circles was etched there, black and magenta lines silhouetted against tawny-white sand.

"Oh, someone probably set a bucket down," he said. But then his eyes wandered farther, and he changed his theory. "No, there are more of them, and they're all different sizes..."

It was true. Every few yards was another grouping of circles within circles, each geometrically perfect; all in black and dark red shades but of different sizes. A puzzled look crossed his face. I continued to rattle on about space ships and aliens, joking in part but completely amazed by whatever force had engineered their creation.

They reminded me of the times when halos form around the sun; a giant ring encircled by a larger and then even a larger one. They might have been rainbows, captured on black and white film, with no horizon to cut them in half. Still again, maybe the dart board at Howard's Pub. What they really looked like, I decided, were the figures I used to make at school in art and math class using a compass and a pencil; doodling we called it.

As we walked along the dune line marvelling at the perfection of the figures on the beach, it became apparent that they all had one thing in common. At the center of each was a piece of grass; a tiny, crumpled inconspicuous piece of eel grass, lodged in the sand. This, it dawned on us, was the explanation. The story of the artwork unfolded before us. The beach, extending from the dunes to the ocean, was the artist's giant canvas. The various kinds of sand were the colors on the artist's palette. The piece of eel grass was the paintbrush. The hand of the artist was the wind, and the artist itself? Mother Nature, wearing the awesome guise of the tempest which had hurled itself upon the island, completed its work, and departed for other shores to the north.

The air was still now and the art show was attended only by the gulls that occasionally passed overhead and by two wandering humans. It was a temporary exhibit anyway; in a few days the circles would be gone. What time and energy, however, must have gone into their creation!

The canvas had been forming for thousands of years, beginning as a hot frothing magma deep under the earth which gradually cooled when it reached the surface into an igneous rock known as quartz. This quartz, far to the west of where it lay today, was ground into tiny grains and transported by streams and rivers to the coast. Here it continued to move, relocated at the whim of the tides and winds as the waters of the Atlantic rose and fell, creating and re-creating the islands we call the Outer Banks. The beach we walked on today was a new creation, far different from the one that had been there before the storm.

The artist's palette—the colors that formed the circles—were made of finer sands, also formed underground and carried many miles, over many years, to the sea. The black hues were probably formed from magnetite and ilmenite, the dark red from garnet.

Lying limp and barely noticed in the sand today, the tiny pieces of eel grass that formed the artist's paintbrushes had once been vital living organisms, an important part of the ecosystem of Pamlico Sound. They had carried on the important business of converting sunlight to chlorophyll and carbon dioxide to oxygen, and providing habitat for scallops, hatchling fish, and other marine animals. But somehow they had been snatched from their estuarine environment and carried by the tides through Hatteras or Ocracoke Inlets into the ocean. They had then been pushed by the waves up the beach to the dunes' edge, where one end had been lodged under the hard, wet sand, ready for the artist.

And then the hand of the artist, the mighty wind, created and empowered by a low pressure system, had seized the piece of eel grass. It had whipped it round and round and round, clockwise and counter-clockwise, using each crook and bend in the grass to paint the concentric rings.

Did the artist, Mother Nature, have a plan as she directed all the processes, over all the years, that led to the formation of these circles? Do they have a purpose, or are they merely the creations of random chance? As I gazed at them one last time they brought to mind the sand paintings of the Navajo Indians. Their medicine men spend hours producing beautiful artwork in the desert, using various colors of sand, as part of healing ceremonies for ailing patients. At the end, they destroy the paintings, brushing the design back into the desert floor. The healing ceremony is complete.

Perhaps the etchings on the beach, soon to be swept away by the wind, were part of a ceremony Mother Nature designed to heal the ailing oceans and earth and to protect her creatures from the dangers that threaten them. Perhaps they were, after all, messages to some-one in the Great Beyond. Maybe they were just doodles in the sand, games she plays with her own specially made compasses. Whatever they may be, the circles in the sand are cause for wonder and awe at the miracles of Nature.

The secret world of
mosquito ditches

Mid-winter had crept up again, clothing me in its exquisite soli-
tude. Each morning before rising I spent a few minutes gazing out
my window. The silent silhouette of a northern harrier, or marsh hawk,
could often be seen sweeping across the salt marsh hunting for its
breakfast. Beyond, where the sound stretches to the horizon and meets
the sky, I watched pelicans glide in formation or buffleheads bob-
bing with the waves. Occasionally a cacophony of honking would
attract my attention and, peering up through the glass, I could see
the powerful strokes of Canada geese as they winged above my house.
Closer by, within a few feet of my window, myrtle or yellow-rumped
warblers scurried busily among the cedar branches, feeding on plump
baby blue berries. One morning I watched their antics come to a
quick halt as a swift, deadly shadow darted into their midst. There
was a brief scuffle; then a glimpse of colorful plumage as an Ameri-
can kestrel, the smallest of our falcons, zoomed away. It was a long
time before the remaining warblers resumed their feeding.

I stopped taking the newspaper, having decided to spend my early
mornings writing. I spent many hours walking with Huck and strum-
ming my guitar. I visited with friends in the evening and read. I also
continued my work with the island's feral cats and, when needed,
with injured birds.

A late winter morning was a good time to be curled up in front of the fire with a cup of coffee, a book, and a gray tabby cat, but I had work to do. I reluctantly pushed Scamp onto the floor, slipped on my heavy coat, and pulled my dip net out of the pile of kayak paddles and shovels. Grabbing the handle of a bucket, I walked over to the creek.

It was a bit cold for this sort of thing, but I could at least give it a try. I leaned over the edge and swung my net down through the water, pulling up a rather gooey mess of algae and?... Nothing. At least not the fish and shrimp I was hoping for. Well, I had figured it was too cold for them to be swimming about. Maybe they were closeted in the mud on the bottom.

I tried again, this time dragging the nylon strands of net through the black, molasses-like mud. When I pulled it up it was full of grass, leaves, unidentified muck, a few small snails, and Yes! wiggling, wriggling little bodies which a closer look told me were the organisms I was seeking. I triumphantly inverted the net over the bucket and took another swipe at the bottom. Success again. When I had a couple dozen shrimp and a few small fish I put the net away, carried the bucket into the house, and ran slightly warm water into my bathtub.

In a cage on the bathroom floor sat the reason I had braved the cold to go dip netting on this gray winter morn. From the cage, I gently lifted a small but beautifully marked duck--a red-breasted merganser drake, known on Ocracoke as a fisherman duck. He had been injured—possibly hit by a car—a few days earlier and brought to me. I had treated him for shock and set his broken foot. This morning I had removed the splint and bandage, and now I wanted to see if he could use the foot. I set the duck in the water and watched as he reveled. He swam, drank, and put his head under the water, obviously searching for something.

"Sorry, guys", I apologized to the shrimp and fish as I scooped some into the tub. I always feel a bit guilty about feeding creatures to other creatures, wondering if I have the right to make the decision of whose life has more value. The merganser was unquestionably glad, however, and proceeded to gobble them up as quickly as I could scoop them in. I was pleased to see that he seemed quite able to maneuver with his damaged foot. A few more days of rest and a few more buckets of creek delicacies and he would be ready to release.

The creek where I netted the shrimp and fish is actually a small canal or, as native Ocracokers say, a "ditch." It was dug, along with a whole network of similar ones throughout the village, during World War II to help control mosquitoes. About 10 feet wide and four feet deep, this one follows the road, crossing under it and joining another canal that leads into Pamlico Sound. At this end it stops near my house in a small pond that once was a home for domestic ducks and geese.

A juncus, or black needlerush, marsh lies on the far side of the creek. Where the creek enters my yard grow marsh cordgrass, broomstraw rush, and cattails. Several wax myrtle trees, a small palmetto, and a number of groundsel or cottonbush shrubs grow alongside it, and between it and the road is a lush stand of seaside goldenrod that turns the roadside wildly yellow in the fall. The waters in the creek are brackish—somewhere between fresh and salt—and they rise and fall in accordance with the daily tides.

A few weeks before, the "Twin Nor'easters of '98" had engorged the creek and surrounding salt marsh until the waters rose up over the banks, spilled into the road and my yard. Mergansers could be seen diving in the foot and a half of water in the road. With their regular routines disturbed, mink, otters, bitterns and rails, which usually remained secreted away in the marsh or the banks of the creek, became for a few days regular sights. The waters had finally receded however, and the creek was back to normal.

What lies within the murky depths of this waterway so near my house has always intrigued me. At the bottom is a gooey substrate of mud and silt covered by decaying leaves and grasses. Bacterial decomposition of this organic detritus depletes the oxygen, leaving hydrogen sulfide, which causes the strong sulfuric "rotten egg" odor I sometimes smell when I pull up my net. On its surface float rather unappealing globs of filamentous or micro-algae, which in too large amounts can choke out the creek, but in small amounts provide food for its inhabitants.

The waters are home, I know, to a number of big snapping turtles, sleeping now, which in the spring put on an amazingly tender and entertaining courtship display. In summer they can sometimes be seen ambling slowly across the road, their rough ridged shells and horned faces looking downright primeval.

Minks also live in the creek, burrowing into dens along its edges and coming out to feed on rodents, birds, and other small creatures. Whether the minks are native or an introduced species, they are well-entrenched residents.

A family of river otters resides here part time, burrowing under the bank and swimming back and forth along the smaller ditch that joins it to the sound. The first time I heard them splashing and squealing I thought they were children, so loud and boisterous were they. Although normally associated with fresh water, river otters thrive here, living off the abundant fish, marsh crabs, and other fauna.

Marsh fiddler crabs hide in holes along the muddy edges of the creek, venturing out to feed and mate. Males use their huge "fiddle claws" to make clicking sounds for courting. The small claws are used for digging and obtaining food.

The mosquitofish and killifish I caught to feed the merganser are plentiful, especially in warm weather. Killifish get their name from the Dutch word for river. They are similar to freshwater minnows, but are chunkier and have squared or rounded tail fins. There are several kinds, but most living in the ditches at Ocracoke are mummichogs. Mummichogs derive their name from an Indian word for "going in crowds," which is exactly what they do.

Mosquitofish, also known as topminnows, are most often seen feeding at the surface, often on mosquito larvae as their name implies. Local knowledge has it that they were introduced when the ditches were dug to help reduce mosquito populations. These small (a maximum of two inches) fish look like guppies and are live bearers.

Small eels—elvers they are called—are among the most fascinating residents of Ocracoke's ditches. On their long migrations from the Sargasso Sea female eels continue inland to fresh water rivers, but many of the males stay on the coast. These snakelike fish are "catadromous," which means they must return to the sea to spawn.

The shrimp, known locally as glass shrimp, are the most prolific of the animals I catch in my net. These small, slender, almost transparent crustaceans belong to the order *Decapoda*, which means "ten legs." They are not the shrimp we humans relish in our cocktails and dinner recipes, but they are popular with other animals.

Also living in the creek are tiny amphipods, which have curved bodies and hard chitinous exoskeletons; isopods, which rather resemble aquatic bugs; and mud snails, which move slowly over the substrate, dining as they go on algae and faunal remains. Innumerable kinds of phyto-(plant) and zoo-(animal) plankton, too small for our eyes to decipher, have a rich community of their own under those dark waters.

Larger ditches and canals on the island are home to various other animals, including diamondback terrapins, blue crabs, hermit crabs, and a variety of fish hatchlings. Each has its unique ecosystem, depending on its size, water salinity, tidal flow, and surrounding environment.

After a few days I released the merganser at the sound, where he would have plenty of space to swim and dive. The creek critters would still provide food for kingfishers and herons, but at least they wouldn't have to worry about that big omnivorous net for a while. I'll continue, however, to reach down occasionally for a swoop of muck, just to see who my neighbors are, and to share with others the fascinating secret world that exists in the barren-looking, molasses-like ditches that intersect Ocracoke Village.

The pintail decoy

Winter was coming to an end, but the cold winds still held the island hostage. Each morning, after starting the coffee and turning on the gas fireplace, I walked down to the nearby soundside beach with Huck and let him run. He loved chasing the gulls and searching through the eel grass for dead fish. I would gaze across the dark pewter waters, trying to identify the waterfowl that bobbed on the waves. I might catch the haunting refrain of a red-throated loon or recognize the distant shapes of mergansers or pintail ducks. I'd follow the tracks left in the sand during the night, trying to decipher the identity of otters, minks, great blue herons, and willets. Often I picked up shells, bones, pieces of wood, or some other odd piece that caught my eye. My house is put together with flotsam and jetsam; discards of the sea and of people who no longer need them. My bathroom walls were once part of a ship that wrecked near Ocracoke. My fence, shelves, and cabinets were built in part with pieces of wood tossed onto the shore by storms and gathered as I roamed the beaches.

Later I might shove my kayak into the back of my truck and drive back to that same beach for a paddle. Oftentimes I'd bring along a bag to pick up trash, or eel grass for my garden. I came to know the winding shoreline of the sound almost as well as the environs of Marsh Haven.

I found it under a pile of eel grass, pushed and rolled up onto the shore in the last nor'easter, wedged against the bank of marshgrass that stopped and entangled it. Just a part of one wing was visible, and I was sure, as I carefully unwrapped it, that it would be broken. But though worn and faded by water and weather, it was in one piece; even its long fragile tail feathers still intact. It was a hunter's decoy, a finely made polyethylene replica of a pintail drake, known locally as a "sprigtail."

I carried it back to my truck and set it on the floorboard, then went back to my task. The last two February storms had piled boards and all kinds of trash onto the soundside beach near my house. I had trucked my kayak out earlier to go paddling, and afterward thought I would fill up the truck bed with the flotsam I found and haul it to the dump. I worked for another half hour or so, picking up all kinds of strange items, but nothing as interesting as the decoy.

I had found others over the years as I explored the marshy shores of Pamlico Sound; a black duck, a mallard, part of a brant. Most were broken, but a few were worth carrying home and setting on my porch. Once one of the local hunters knocked on my door and claimed my find, showing me where his mark on the bottom identified it as his. I looked carefully at this one for identifying marks, so I could return it to its owner; but the scratches on it were haphazard and meaningless.

Sometimes while kayaking in hunting season I would see decoys where they had been set out and left to attract waterfowl. Sometimes there would be ducks or geese swimming with them, and it would be hard at first to tell the difference between the plastic models and the living birds. I would paddle slowly and watch, snapping some photographs if I had my camera; but I left these decoys where they were, to be retrieved by their rightful owner.

Ocracoke and nearby islands were a mecca for duck and goose hunters in the early part of this century, and guiding hunting trips was an important means of earning a living in the winter. Hunt clubs such as Green Island and Quork Hammock Clubs attracted sportsmen from all over the east, and Ocracoke was described by Rex Beach in his book *Oh Shoot!* as the center of the goose-hunting industry. Live decoys were often used then, as well as ones hand-carved from wood or fashioned by stretching canvas over a wood frame. Old-time Ocracoke hunting guides such as Clinton Gaskill and Fowler O'Neal, remember making their own decoys. Hunters hid in low, well-disguised batteries as they waited to attract wild waterfowl.

Batteries and live decoys are illegal today. Ocracokers now hunt from stake blinds, wooden structures that can be seen in the shallows of Pamlico Sound, and from shore blinds made with myrtle branches and marsh grass. There are still a few professional guides, but most Ocracokers just hunt for themselves and their families. They frequently use plastic decoys like the one I had found to lure live ducks down. This one had most likely spent a lot of time floating with real pintails before being kidnapped by the wind and sea and stashed away in the eel grass.

American or Northern Pintails (*Anas acuta*) are common winter residents in the waters surrounding Ocracoke. Watching with binoculars from the shore or from my kayak, I often see them fly between the salt marsh and the reefs where they feed. They are large ducks, reaching a length of up to 29 inches, with slender bodies, long necks, and long pointed wings. Males are adorned in soft colors of grey, white, brown, and black, with the distinctive long tail feathers that give them their name. Females are mostly brown and resemble female mallards. More common in the west than the east, the pintails' range extends over all of North America. Described by naturalist Herbert K. Job in 1917 as "the greyhound among waterfowl," they are graceful and swift, and have been clocked flying at 65 miles per hour.

Pintails are known, along with mallards, teals, and shovelers, as "puddle-ducks" or "dabbling" ducks. They feed by turning tail-up in shallow waters to reach aquatic plants and invertebrates. They do not dive for food, but may to escape detection. They are graceful on land and are able to spring immediately into flight.

On this day in late February most had probably already departed on their long migration north, where they would mate and nest in the tundras of Alaska. After raising a brood of six to nine young they would be ready to return, and would appear again at Ocracoke in rafts of several hundred next fall.

As I rinsed the decoy and tried to shake out the water, I was reminded of an old book I had recently brought down from my parents' attic. *The Velveteen Rabbit or How Toys Become Real*, written in 1922 by Margery Williams Bianco, is the story of a stuffed velveteen rabbit who longs to jump and run with the wild rabbits he sees in the garden. They talk to him and ask him to join them; then they laugh when they find he has no back legs to hop with. But one day, after he has grown old and shabby and is lying discarded in a bag of trash outdoors, a tear he sheds becomes a flower, and the flower a magic fairy, who turns him into a real rabbit. He joins the wild rabbits in the garden and, in the way of storybooks, lives happily ever after.

Did the wild pintails, I wonder, try to talk to my decoy when they flew down from the sky to float beside it? Did they wonder why it didn't swim along the shore, dip its head beneath the water to feed, or rise in flight when a movement in the marsh startled them? Did they notice that it had no legs for swimming, or that its wings were fashioned tightly to his sides so that it could not fly? Did they laugh at it or pity it?

What about the worn decoy I held in my hands? Had it, like the velveteen rabbit, watched the wild ones and longed to join them in their antics; to rise from the water and fly away across the horizon? Did it, too, yearn to be real? And did it know why it had been set out to float there in the sound? Had it tried to warn the wild pintails "No! Stay away! It's a trap!" but, unable to cry alarm, watched the brothers it envied die around it?

"It's just a plastic decoy," I reminded myself, "and this is no fairytale. I'll set it on my porch shelf, along with the other treasures I have collected on the beach. Maybe its original owner will claim it, or it can serve as a reminder of this day and the lovely wild ducks I so often see from the beach."

Or maybe...I muse...just maybe some day I'll take it back and set it down in the sound, so that a mermaid-like fairy can cast a spell and make it real, and it can join the wild pintails as they fly north for the summer.

The happy clown

The reasons I love Ocracoke are not all related to the sea, the sound, and the marsh. Ocracoke has a sense of community that is not found in many places. An unspoken but deep-seated assumption exists that if someone needs something, someone will be there for them. There is no one on the island I would not turn to for help, or to whom I would not, in turn, offer help. Conflicts and disagreements develop at times, as they do anywhere, as well as petty arguments and hurtful gossip. But the bond between islanders is strong, and that strength is seated in Ocracoke's tradition as an independent, self-reliant, sea-faring community.

Besides the support of the community as a whole, I feel privileged to have especially close ties with a number of good friends, both male and female. As long as they are here I know that I need never be alone at Ocracoke.

Yet through the years I have lived here, both at Marsh Haven and before, the one constant that has remained true in my life has been a sense of aloneness. It is not necessarily a bad thing. Solitude can be the key that opens the spirit to oneness with nature; loneliness the knife that sharpens the pencil of creativity. Overcoming the pain of aloneness, learning not only to live with it but to find joy in it, is one of life's great challenges.

The world is so full of a number of sounds
I am sure we should all be as happy as clowns.

Well, it's not exactly Robert Louis Stevenson, but this was the thought that came to mind as I sat on my porch swing early one morning in late April.

I had awakened at seven to near darkness and a gusty wind that was driving rain through my bedroom window and soaking me and my bed. *Just what I need*, I thought. I was already feeling blue about losing a good friend; and here I was faced with a morning so dismal and gray that I had to turn on the overhead lights to convince Huck that it was time to get up.

Glumly I made my coffee and fed the cats, wondering what I could do to lift my spirits on this gloomy Saturday. First decision of the day: Where shall I drink my coffee? *Well*, I thought rather facetiously as I glanced out the window, *If you can't beat it, join it*!

So I turned off the radio (a rock & roll station I had flipped on to help brighten my mood), gathered up a blanket, and took my cup of coffee out on my wrap-around porch. Now I was surrounded by the full intensity of the storm. I sat for a few minutes, my eyes closed, and listened.

A full symphony was in progress, and what an eclectic assemblage of musicians! The wind, spawned by thermal drafts and air movement into areas of low pressure, was clearly the chief orchestrater. It conducted melodious sonatas in the grasses of the salt marsh. If you listened carefully you could hear varying pitches as the wind played the assorted strings of the different kinds of grass that make up the marsh ecosystem.

It plucked the stiff cylindrical leaves of *Juncus roemerianus*, or black needlerush, the primary plant of the upper intertidal marsh, to create a soft tapping sound. The flat grainlike blades of Spartina alterniflora, or marsh cordgrass, which forms the basis of the lower intertidal zone, rustled softly as the bow of the wind stroked its strings. The tall dry stalks of last year's cattails (*Typha latifolia*)—a freshwater reed unusual in a salt marsh like this—sounded a bit like tambourines as they clattered raggedly on the other side of my hammock. The wind didn't just play strings; it turned the crevices in my house into saxophones and clarinets as it channeled its breath through them, changing notes each time it changed direction.

The pelting drops of rain, squeezed out of the storm clouds by cooling and condensation, played rhythm along with the wind: steady drumbeats as it pounded the roof, a softer percussion as it pattered the grass, tympanic splashes as it landed on the water in the creek. Then echoed the sound of trombones in the distant thunder rumbling against the clouds, ending with an eerie silence that if you listened carefully, was not silence at all but the faraway ebb and flow of the ocean playing its own dramatic concert a mile away.

The ensemble of musicians was accompanied by the wild noisy gyrations of dancers. The shaggy arms of the cedar trees (*juniperus virginiana*), whirled in all directions, keeping time with the frantic rhythm of the wind as they waved their emerald skirts in abandon. The needles rustled against the house, and one branch tapped out a staccato drumbeat on my roof. Beneath them a branch of wax myrtle (*Myrica cerifera*) slapped its own andante tempo against the screen, shedding the last of its berries, a popular winter feast for the warblers, onto the ground.

And then, lovely as any of Mozart's flute concertos, there trilled a duet performed by two red-winged blackbirds staking out their homestead rights in song. They produced their music by forcing air from their lungs across an elastic membrane in their syrinx, an organ similar to our larynx. When the membrane vibrated, stretching and tightening, different tones resulted. Oblivious of the storm, a pair of mockingbirds and a boat-tailed grackle joined in, creating a symphony fit for royalty. I was quite sure that the London Philharmonic, attended by the queen herself, could not outdo this performance, and here I sat with a private viewing and front row seat. It was at this point that my version of Stevenson's lyrics popped into my head.

It's true, I thought to myself, opening my eyes. Robert Louis Stevenson was right when he composed his poem over a hundred years ago. Included in his collection *A Child's Garden of Verses*, it has an important message for everyone, be he seven or 70.

In his version, "The world is so full of a number of things, I am sure we should all be as happy as kings," the "things" he refers to are available to everyone, but they are as wonderful as the riches owned by any king. We often miss them in the hustle and bustle of our daily lives, closing our minds and our hearts as we embrace our own private sorrows and troubles. We forget to look beyond the struggles that are part of being human and accept the simple gifts that nature offers us. These gifts—the whistle of the wind, the rustle of grasses, the trilling of a mockingbird—are treasures each and every one, and they should in fact make us happier than kings, for they are freely given.

But now the wind had shifted west and was blowing the rain onto the porch and onto me. I was getting sopping wet, and besides, my coffee cup was empty. So I went back into my darkened house, only now it did not seem gloomy and sad. Nature, even in her most glum and threatening form, possesses a magical presence which can elate my spirits if I give it a chance. I felt inspired by the world-class performance I had just experienced, enriched by the pearls and sapphires of sound that had dazzled my senses.

I would tuck a few of these jewels into the pockets of my memory, and if I could not be as happy as a king, or even a clown, all day long, every once in a while I would reach down into that pocket and remind myself that they were there.

A visitor in the night: the hermit crab

Spring was rounding the corner again, heading in leaps and bounds towards summer, rental season, and time for me to move out of Marsh Haven again. I had made a momentous decision during the past few months. I determined to stop worrying about the little day-to-day problems of life; to take more risks; to live with more passion. I had, after all, no children or husband to worry about. Huck and my cats were my main responsibility, and I would keep their welfare in mind. The immediate result of my decision was to quit my job at the Fig Tree. It was not that I did not like it. I enjoyed being with my friends and the work was usually fun. But it did not allow me enough time to do the things that I felt truly passionate about, like writing. The worst that could happen, I rationalized, was that I would lose what money I had and, ultimately (though not probably; I have more faith in life than that) Marsh Haven. In that case, I would be right back where I was four years earlier, and I would just have to start over. I had done that before. Okay, so I would keep driving my 14-year-old truck, recycling used aluminum foil, buying wine with screw caps instead of corks. I could handle it.

My decision brought an exhilarating sense of freedom; a feeling that if you had nothing you were afraid to lose, you were free to try anything, to do anything. With the extra time that I had bequeathed myself, I spent more hours doing things that I loved and believed in. It seemed to work just fine.

Nighttime lay like a feather quilt on my little house, enveloping me and mine in an aura of comfort. I had taken my shower, eaten my supper, and now lay curled up in bed with a copy of Pat Conroy's *Beach Music.* Huck was stretched out at the foot of the bed, Squirt curled up on her pillow, Miss Kelley on my stomach; and Scamp watched from the shelf, fastidiously washing her foot.

I was enjoying the pleasant exhaustion inspired by a day out-doors, working in my garden in the morning and later taking a long walk on the beach. It had been a sunny, cloudless day, hot for early summer at Ocracoke, but pleasant and relaxing. I had picked up a few shells as I walked along, tucking them into my pockets for later perusal. Now, hours later, I was beginning to drift into the nether world of dreams.

Suddenly I heard a noise, a scratching sound. With three cats living in the house and 10 formerly feral ones outside, I was accus-tomed to strange noises and usually tried to ignore them. This one however, was obviously coming from downstairs, inside the house, and my indoor crew was accounted for. I started to feel uneasy. There it was again, apparently in the kitchen. I wondered if it could be a giant cockroach, what I prefer to call a palmetto or water bug. Maybe a mouse, or (Oh no!) a rat?

Huck listened with his ears raised, but was too lazy to get up. I climbed out of bed and crept down the stairs toward the sound, then quickly flipped on the overhead light, expecting to catch the culprit in action. I saw nothing, however, out of the ordinary. No cockroach, no mouse, no rat; just the pile of miscellaneous beach items I had taken out of my pocket and set on the kitchen counter. Puzzled, I turned off the light and went back upstairs.

I had no sooner gotten settled when I heard it again; scritch-scratch, scritch-scratch. Again I crept down the stairs, watching carefully. Then I saw it; a movement on the counter. As I stood there I noticed that one of the shells I had found, a beige and white gastropod known as a moon shell, was moving! Slowly it worked its way across the marble surface, approaching the edge. Just in time I went into action and rescued it from a fall, and as I did I caught a glimpse of waving claws. The shell I had picked up was the mobile home of a hermit crab.

Hermit crabs are common residents of coastal waters along the eastern United States, found in both the ocean and in sounds and bays. They are seldom actually seen in full, however, for they live in the vacated shells of gastropods, such as this moon shell. When not withdrawn in hiding, their two large claws, legs, antennae, and stalked eyes are visible as they walk along the shallows, hunting for food.

They are not true crabs but belong, along with the Alaskan king crab, to the infraorder *Anomura*, having four rather than five pairs of well-developed legs. Out of their shells they more closely resemble lobsters than crabs. Their long curved abdomens are soft and vulnerable, which is why they seek protection in gastropod shells.

Like shrimp, lobsters, and true crabs, they belong to the scientific order *Decapoda*, which is Greek for "10 feet." They are Crustaceans: invertebrates with segmented bodies, jointed appendages, a pair of cutting or crushing mandibles, and hard outer shells (or exoskeletons) made of chitin on part of their bodies. They breathe through gills and have compound eyes that sit on stalks.

Like other decapods, they go through several stages in their lives. Mating takes place immediately after the female sheds and lasts about an hour and a half. Hundreds of eggs are fertilized by the male's spermatophores and become attached to the female's abdomen, where they develop for 12 days. They hatch into large-eyed, free-swimming larvae known as zoea, which bear little resemblance to adult crabs. The zoea develop into postlarvae known as glaucothoe, which are free-swimming at first but soon find a deserted mollusk shell into which they move. They continue to shed and develop into adult hermit crabs.

Hermit crabs are totally dependent on the mollusk shells they live in and are constantly on the search for new ones. As they grow and shed they must find larger shells to fit their needs. They have roughened file-like surfaces on their terminal appendages, the uropods, which they press against the inner sides of their shells to help them hold on.

Several species of hermit crabs are found in the coastal waters of North Carolina. The largest is the Giant Hermit Crab, which can be four and a half inches long and often inhabits whelk shells. The Long-clawed Hermit Crab, a small crab about a half inch long, is the most commonly found species. It lives in periwinkle, oyster drill, and mud snail shells. Light refractions cause the eyes of the Star-eyed Hermit Crab, a medium-sized crab, to resemble star sapphires. The crab on my countertop was probably either a Striped or a Flat-clawed, both medium-sized crabs often found above the water line.

I was not happy about discovering a hermit crab on my countertop. I knew that the marine species that live at Ocracoke, different from the Caribbean land crabs sold in shops, could not survive for long away from the water. It would probably not make it till morning, and here it was 11 at night with me in my nightgown. I would have to change my clothes, drive to the beach parking lot, climb over the dunes, and hike back to the water's edge. That was preferable, however, to finding the crab curled up dead in the morning. So I called Huck and we hopped in my pickup truck, and were soon back at the beach road.

Leaving the truck at the parking lot, we walked across the ramp that traversed the rolling dunes. The sand shimmered in the moonlight and the Atlantic Ocean stretched endlessly to the east. I set the shell down at the water's edge, its tiny resident hiding inside, and gazed around me. The night was breathtaking, and I was suddenly glad that the hermit crab had unwittingly brought me out to enjoy it.

Thoughts of Ocracoke from afar

When I moved out of Marsh Haven for the 1998 rental season I had no specific plans in mind. I wanted to spend some time with my family in Virginia and do some serious writing, but I felt the need to do something else as well. I had spent a good part of my younger years flitting here and there about the countryside, "foot-loose and fancy free," so to speak. I had roamed through this and other countries, hitch-hiking, crewing on sailboats, riding third-class trains, stopping and getting jobs whenever I needed money. But it had been a long time since I had done anything like that. Having decided that I wanted to live life with more passion and risk, I reasoned that this was the time to start.

I thought about going back out west, visiting the people and places I had enjoyed in the years I had lived there. But what I needed, I decided instead, was to go somewhere new; a place I knew nothing about, where I knew no one. It would need to be a place where I could take Huck and Miss Kelley, since they were both a bit too rowdy for my family to keep. That eliminated overseas countries with pet quarantine regulations. I didn't have a lot of money saved up, so it couldn't be a plush, expensive place. I am absolutely petrified of traveling in cities, particularly in an old, oil-guzzling truck that might break down at any time, so that eliminated several routes. It didn't take me long to decide where I wanted to go, and having made my choice, it took even less time to get on the road.

I'm sitting here waiting for the ferry, as I've done hundreds of times before—sometimes the one connecting Ocracoke Island and Swan Quarter or Cedar Island, more often the one to Hatteras. This time, however, I'm on a rocky beach in Newfoundland, Canada, and the ferry I'm waiting for is bound for Labrador. It seems as if I've ridden a lot of ferries to get here; a medium-size one across Lake Champlain from New York to Vermont; a small one from Prince Edward Island to Nova Scotia; an even smaller one across St. Ann's Bay in Cape Breton; a huge one across a hundred miles of Atlantic Ocean to Newfoundland; and now....

The boat to Labrador doesn't leave until morning, so I've camped out here for the evening. Huck is eagerly exploring the piles of driftwood and abandoned lobster traps, hoping to find some tasty tidbits. Miss Kelley is peering over the dashboard of the truck, watching every move he makes. I'm sitting in front of a small campfire, waiting for a half dozen Atlantic mackerel I caught yesterday to turn sizzling hot and brown on the grill I positioned over it. And to tell the truth, I'm feeling pretty pleased with myself....

I didn't really expect to make it this far when I set out on my journey five weeks earlier. My ultimate goal, I informed everyone, was Labrador; but I figured either my money, my truck, or my courage would give out somewhere before I got there. My truck has been behaving beautifully and seems quite happy as long as I feed her gasoline and quarts of oil simultaneously every couple hundred miles. My money...well, that might have slowed things down except for that miracle of modern times, the credit card (I'll worry about the bill later.) As for my courage, that has faltered a few times, I admit.

Huck and Kelley are great company, but neither of them has a drivers license to help while away the miles, and their conversational abilities are somewhat limited (back to school for them when I get back!). But here I sit at the gateway to Labrador, and as I gaze across the Straits of Belle Isle at the mist-enshrouded silhouette of that great Arctic wilderness, I feel, as I said, rather pleased with myself.

I have to admit though, as far as I've traveled, I never completely left home. Bits and pieces of Ocracoke keep showing up along the way. I'm not just referring to the Carolina sand that I find throughout my truck, no matter how many times I clean it out. I'm not talking about the many rust spots on the truck's recently painted exterior, the results of Ocracoke's moist and salty environment. I'm not referring to the white chalk marks on my tires, friendly reminders from the National Park Service not to leave my truck in their parking lot for too long while out boating.

It's more than that. Ocracoke is lodged firmly in my thoughts, and I am reminded of her by many of the things I see along the way. In Rangely, Maine, for example, I stopped for a week, discouraged by the rain that insisted on falling every day, and got a temporary job. The Pub and Grub where I cooked made me think of Ocracoke's Howard's Pub which, though larger, is very similar. I doctored scrapes on my hands not so different from those sported by Howard's Pub employees. But whereas theirs were caused by shucking oysters, mine came from cracking and cleaning big, bright-red Maine lobsters.

While in Maine I watched loons as they swam and dove serenely in their summer homes on the state's many lakes. Those were some of the same loons, I realized, that spent last winter in Ocracoke with me. They were wearing the soft browns and grays of their winter plumage then, but now were dressed in their Sunday best: bright black-and-white tuxedos with black bow ties. They swam lower in the water here, and I wondered if it was because the fresh lake water has less buoyancy than Ocracoke's salty brine. Their cries had a different sound as well, and I remembered that up here in their breeding grounds they had reason to use their "tremolo" mating songs and the "hoots" with which they talked to their babies.

After leaving Maine I headed for Canada. While on Prince Edward Island, I picked up a guide at the visitors center, and one of the first things I saw when I opened it up was a story about P.E.I's famous piping plovers. *Wait a minute!* I thought. *They're not THEIR piping plovers. They're OUR piping plovers!* I had often ridden the beaches of Ocracoke as a Volunteer in the Park counting, observing, and documenting the nesting success of these endangered shore birds.

I stopped at Prince Edward National Park to talk with the rangers and we compared notes about the plovers. The main predators there were foxes and hawks, whereas cats, minks, and gulls attacked the nests at Ocracoke. The Prince Edward rangers built enclosures to protect them, something we do not normally do. They averaged 25 nesting pairs a summer, whereas Ocracoke, which lies at the southern limit of their range, had less than a dozen. In both places, however, loss of nesting habitat due to human encroachment is threatening their chances of survival, and we agreed that cooperation between Canada and the United States was of utmost importance. They offered to send me what information they had so I could share it with the Ocracoke rangers.

Throughout the Maritimes, as the Atlantic Coast provinces of Canada are often called, I have found myself intrigued by the fisheries. I am sure I must have been a commercial fisherman in some previous life. I am constantly drawn to the harbors, where I visit with the fishermen and compare stories. "Yes, we have scallops too, but we harvest the bay scallops at Ocracoke, which are smaller than these."

"No, we don't have any cod. Fishermen catch flounder, blues, and drum, to name a few. We have mackerel, but they're spanish mackerel, not Atlantic—very different." "No, no lobster in Carolina. Nope, I'm not kidding. We have blue crab, which are delicious, but not one lobster. We do have some mighty tasty shrimp down there, though."

One day when I was on the west coast of Prince Edward Island, in a little village called Skinners Pond, I was chatting with one of the fishermen, comparing notes and asking about what they were catching that day. Things were slow in general, with their quota for lobster already filled. "They're bringing in a few halibut," he told me, "some mackerel and hake. And then of course there are the mossers."

"Mossers?" I inquired, displaying my abysmal ignorance. "Are they a kind of fish?"

He laughed. "No, you know, mossers. They bring in the Irish moss."

Well, I didn't know, and my confusion showed in my face. Could "Irish moss" be anything like the Spanish moss that hangs in curtains from some of the live oaks in Ocracoke?

"Irish moss," he explained, "is a kind of seaweed. Here. I'll show you. Jim just brought in a load." We walked over to a pick-up truck and peered in the back. It was full, as he had said, of seaweed. He showed me the rakes on the back of the boat, docked nearby, which had been used to collect it. Well, here was one fishery with which Ocracoke had nothing to compare. I was intrigued.

I remembered what Mrs. Keye, the elderly woman whose boarding house I was staying at, had said when I asked her about her large, beautiful draft horses. "They're mossin' horses," she had told me. I didn't know what she meant, but I was having trouble understanding

187

her accent already, so I didn't pursue it. Now I went back and asked her. After a big northwest blow, she explained, the beaches in West Prince were piled high with Irish moss. The islanders hitched specially made rakes to the horses and rode them through the shallow surf and sand to gather it up. They transported it to a factory in nearby Miminigash, where it was dried, baled, and shipped to Copenhagen, Denmark.

I longed to see them at work, and luck was with me. That night there was a terrible "thunder squall." It woke Huck, Miss Kelley, and me up and it soaked the inside of my camper shell, which has a mysterious, unidentifiable leak. But the next morning the beaches of West Prince were alive with islanders using hand and horse-drawn rakes, collecting the valuable Irish moss.

I visited the factory in Miminigash and they gave me a tour of the operations. They explained the moss's many uses, such as an additive for ice cream and gelatin. I even tried a piece of "seaweed pie" served at a little restaurant across the road. I wondered if Ocracoke had any kind of seaweed that could be harvested for profit. Eel grass used to be collected and used to stuff mattresses and other furniture, and it is still used locally as a mulch and fertilizer for gardens. Did it have any other, perhaps undiscovered uses? I decided to investigate when I returned home.

On the east coast of "New Scotland" (Nova Scotia), I found tough little island horses that roam free just as the Ocracoke ponies used to do. Their history and physique is amazingly similar to that of the Outer Banks ponies. Nova Scotia also has its share of pirate stories. Liverpool saw a raging battle between Canadian and American privateers in the late eighteenth century, and one ship, the *Liverpool Packet,* captured over a hundred vessels. None of their tales can compare, though, at least in my opinion, to our good old Blackbeard with his flaming beard!

Then there are the accents. Something about the isolation of islands creates and preserves the most wonderful dialects and phraseologies, many of them left over from the "old country." The ancestors of the Maritime Islanders were French Acadians, Scottish Highlanders, and Irishmen. Gaelic and French are still spoken, as well as several variations of English. They are different from the Ocracoke "hoi toide" brogue, but are also colorful, musical, and sometimes hard to understand. "Be yer daeg crass?" was one that took me a while to figure out. Finally I learned to smile and shake my head. "No he's not cross at all. You can pet him if you like."

New Brunswick is pretty; Prince Edward charming; Nova Scotia lovely; but it is Newfoundland that has stolen my heart. Newfoundland reminds me of the Ocracoke I fell in love with when I first moved there. It has a raw beauty, a rough honesty, a feeling of freedom seldom found elsewhere. It is not an easy place to live. Winter lasts for eight months, with temperatures frequently dipping to 30° and 40° below. Most houses are heated only with wood, and land travel is often by skidoo, a small snowmobile. Icebergs make water travel hazardous, and water temperatures are so cold, I am told, that if a man goes overboard, he has three to five minutes before he will freeze to death. And hardest of all, the cod, that seemingly inexhaustible source of sustenance and livelihood on Newfoundland's famous Grand Banks, are nearly gone. With no way to make a living, many of Newfoundland's proud seafaring men are forced to rely on unemployment checks or leave their homes. I hope and pray that Ocracoke's fishing community, also in decline, will fare better.

A week has now passed since I sat waiting for the ferry and writing the paragraphs above. I caught the ferry to Labrador and spent most of the trip being seasick (another reminder of some of my

Ocracoke experiences). These were, after all, rough waters, not far from where the Titanic went down. I followed the road in Labrador for as far as it went. Only boat or dog sled could go farther. The last stop was Red Bay, once a thriving Basque whaling center where the residents had killed, processed, and begun the drive toward extinction of the great right and bowhead whales. One day I hope to go back and ride the freight boat that follows the Labrador coast far to the north to villages that have never seen automobiles or electricity. But for now, my trip was over.

On the ferry back to Newfoundland I met a writer, Paul, a naturalized Canadian citizen originally from the United States, now living in Nova Scotia. His specialty was travel books and brochures. He had visited and written about interesting and beautiful places in many areas of the world. We talked for a while, and when the inevitable question came up, "Where was I from?" I told him I lived on a little island off the coast of North Carolina called Ocracoke. I was surprised to learn that he knew it; had been there, in fact, only weeks before. "Ocracoke! That's one of the most wonderful places anywhere." he said. "Why on earth would you want to leave it?" I smiled. "Well, I wouldn't, at least not for too long."

I am sitting now on yet another ferry, traveling southwest from Yarmouth, Nova Scotia, to Bar Harbor, Maine. Ocracoke has never been far from my thoughts as I traveled, and now, as I head homeward, I think of it more and more. I have had some fascinating, unforgettable experiences, and I've seen some incredibly beautiful places. But wonderful as Maine, Nova Scotia, and Newfoundland are, no place is more wonderful than the little Outer Banks island that I call home. And when I remember that, I feel pleased with myself once again.

The storm bird

I have discovered in the nine years that I have called Ocracoke home that it is far more distressing to endure a hurricane from afar than to be right here. It is not that I crave danger, or that I really believe I can hold off the effects of a major storm. Somehow though, experiencing it does not seem quite as bad as hearing about it on the Weather Channel. I feel just plain unfaithful leaving my cats, trees, and birds to fend for themselves. At any rate, whenever I am off the island and hear about a hurricane brewing I start fretting to get back. Which is just what I did when the weathermen started talking about Hurricane Bonnie in late August of 1998. The way they talked, it was going to be one heck of a killer storm, and every time they showed it on the weather map it appeared to be heading straight for Ocracoke.

I had returned to Richmond two weeks earlier from Canada's Atlantic provinces but still had another month before I could move back to Marsh Haven. So I made plans to deliver a car to Seattle, Washington, an almost free means of getting to the west coast, where I needed to empty out a storage unit. As my scheduled departure and Hurricane Bonnie's predicted landfall drew closer and closer together, I fretted more and more. The morning before I was to start my cross-country trip I awoke to announcements that Ocracoke was being evacuated. My decision was made, seemingly without my participation. I started throwing things into my truck and within an hour

Huck and I were Ocracoke bound.

Hurricane Bonnie was bearing down on the North Carolina coast, pummeling the sea with winds of 115 miles per hour, extending her long arm of terror for 400 miles. Along the coast strings of cars, trucks, and campers wound their way slowly away from her path under orders for mandatory evacuation. Those who stayed behind boarded up windows, tied down boats, and stocked up on candles and food. No one knew where she would come ashore, but everyone was prepared for the worst. Meanwhile, as she made her slow, tortuous trek up the coast, her driving winds and capricious gusts cajoled the ocean into a froth of angry waves.

Somewhere out there, far from land, a graceful, gull-like bird struggled to survive the storm. Known commonly as a Cory's Shearwater, it was about 16 inches long and softly colored in grey-brown tones that blended into white on its underside. Its distinguishing feature was its yellowish beak, or "tubenose," with external, tube-like nostrils. Shearwaters, along with their cousins the petrels and albatrosses, are pelagic birds. They make their homes upon the sea and spend almost all their time on the wing, approaching land only to breed and raise their young. Some of the world's great wanderers, they migrate from ocean to ocean. This one was perhaps on its way north from the islands of the east Atlantic or the Mediterranean, where Cory's shearwaters commonly nest.

The scientific family name for shearwaters and petrels, *Procellariidae*, comes from the Latin word for storm, since according to Pearson's *Birds of America*, they are never found on land unless driven there by one. Now this shearwater was at the mercy of Hurricane Bonnie.

Somehow it was swept up in one of her gusts and carried toward Ocracoke. It fought to escape, beating its slender wings against the relentless wind, but grew gradually weaker. Finally it was dropped against a dune where, as it lay exhausted, swirling sand partially buried it. It was doomed now, a victim of the storm's awesome force.

After a day and a half of wind and rain, Friday morning dawned crisp and clear. The hurricane had moved on, leaving Ocracoke relatively unharmed. The stir-crazy residents came out to assess the damage and enjoy the day. Rufus Weidemeyer, one of the people who had not evacuated, went walking on the beach with his black and tan rotweiller, Jake. He spied something buried in the sand and, moving closer, found that it was a bird. Not knowing what he should do with it, he stopped two women as they passed by. The three of them gently uncovered the small feathered form, limp and helpless, and carried it to the women's jeep.

I was in front of my house mending my picket fence, blown down by the wind, when the blue jeep pulled up. Having made my way to Marsh Haven to ride out the storm, I was happy to have so little damage. After being away for most of the summer, I also was pleased to see my friends, Cynthia Mitchell and Ann Ehringhaus, when they drove up.

"Guess what we brought you," said Cynthia, as she unwrapped a towel from the small bundle in her lap, explaining that Rufus had found the bird. "It seems to have a broken wing," she said, and I agreed.

With the island closed down, I did not have access to an x-ray machine, so I had to guess. Both wings hung loosely when I picked it up, indicative of irreparable joint fractures. The bird was obviously exhausted, barely able to hold up its head or walk. My first inclination was to put the poor creature out of its suffering. Maybe though, I thought, just maybe, it was the exhaustion, rather than fractures, that caused it to hold its wings like that.

"Let's give it a chance."

I gave the shearwater electrolyte fluids through a rubber tube that I ran into its stomach, a process known as gavaging. I placed it in a cage and covered it with a cloth to keep it dark. Then I waited. By the next day it seemed stronger but had no inclination to move. It was quite fat, which indicated that it had been healthy before the storm pushed it inland. (Supposedly shearwaters store enough fat to be used as lanterns.) I switched to a liquid feeding formula, tubing it four times a day. Meanwhile, I studied my bird books, trying to learn more about it.

Shearwaters get their common name from the way they gracefully shear the waves, riding air currents only inches above the water. They scoop up fish, squid, and crustaceans or make short dives and swim with their wings to catch their prey. Living up to 30 years, they show no noticeable differentiation between the sexes. In early summer they congregate on certain islands where each female lays a single egg, using burrows and rock crevices as nests. Both parents help to feed and raise the nestling.

Each day the shearwater grew stronger, and it now held its wings in a normal position. I took it down to the shore of Pamlico Sound and set it in the water in hopes that it would try to fly. Each time it would hightail it back to shore as fast as it could go, shuffling along on its awkwardly set webbed feet. It showed no inclination to use its wings and seemed much more inclined to nestle into my arms than to fly away to sea. (This behavior I attributed to the fact that shearwaters, when on land, nest in burrows.)

Meanwhile, life was returning to normal on the island. The water in the streets dried up and people cleared the debris out of their yards. Shops and restaurants re-opened, and tourists slowly filtered back. I replaced the screens that had blown out of my porch and raked the yard. It would soon be time for me to leave again.

I began to lose hope that the shearwater could ever be released. Perhaps it had a hairline fracture that, while undetectable, made flight impossible; perhaps some neurological damage to its spine or head; maybe irreversible emotional trauma. Whatever the reason, it seemed to have forgotten that it was a pelagic, sea-going bird, or even a bird at all.

Then one night as I sat reading in my window-seat, shortly after sundown, I heard a noise out on the porch. I went out to check and found the shearwater pacing restlessly in its cage, the first such activity it had displayed. I let it out on the porch and watched as it opened its wings and stretched them out, beating them slowly back and forth. Good! Maybe it was getting better.

"I'll take you back down to the sound in the morning," I said with renewed hope. Then I put the bird back in its cage, covered it carefully so that the light would not keep it awake, and went back to my book.

After a few minutes, however, I heard noises again. The shearwater was more restless than before, banging at the cage walls so hard that I was afraid it would hurt itself.

I had never taken a bird out at night, but I decided to give it a try. As we drew near the sound, I realized that a strong wind was coming off the water. Hurricane Danielle was passing offshore, I remembered, and while not close enough to cause us a problem, it was producing strong surf and small craft warnings. Indeed, the dark surface of the estuary was highlighted with whitecaps, and small waves crashed against the shore.

I set the bird in the sand. It sat there for a moment, then scurried toward the water and sat down again, the waves just tickling its breast feathers. Suddenly it ran into the waves. I saw its wings rise and begin beating, and a moment later it was soaring above the water. I watched the ghostly form turn into a dark silhouette and then melt into the night as it flew out across the sound. It was free!

I sat for a moment, gazing across the water, surprised and happy. What had come over it, after so many days of lethargy, to suddenly decide, on this dark windy night, that it was time to go? What had called it? What secret message had it received, and how? Soon the shearwater would be back in its own environment, a place where land was seldom more that a distant shadow on the horizon. I tried to imagine living a life where "home" was an updraft of wind; where you never stayed in one place; where even the waters where you rested were in constant motion.

What had beckoned the shearwaters, petrels, and other pelagic birds back to the sea? They had originated there, along with all life; but millions of years ago their avian ancestors had, with the mammals, moved onto the land. Something drew them back. Was it the same thing, I wondered, that called to the whales and the dolphins? Is it that same ancient urge that summons certain people to the sea to be sailors, roaming from port to port, never settling down in one place?

Returning home, I took my bird books off the shelf again and searched for an explanation for the shearwater's behavior. I saw nothing in the chapters on shearwaters, but in reading about their cousins, the albatrosses, I thought I found what I was looking for. According to *The Birder's Hand-book* (Ehrlich, Dobkin, & Wheye), these birds cannot take off in calm air, but only by running across water into a head wind. Somehow the shear-water had known. Though there was no wind that night on my tree-enshrouded porch, and cer-tainly none in its cloth-enclosed cage, it knew that out on the beach Hur-ricane Danielle had set the stage for its release. It let me know, and thank goodness I had the sense to listen. Had I waited till morning, a lovely, still day when the sound looked like a sea of glass, it would probably never have opened its wings.

The shearwater was indeed a bird of the storm, as its name implied. Brought to Ocracoke by Hurricane Bonnie, it was reclaimed by Danielle and returned, on the pathway of her winds, to its home on the sea.

Of frog legs and crab cakes

When I decided that I wanted to become a wildlife rehabilitator,
back in 1990, I pictured myself cheerfully saving the lives of all kinds
of wild creatures, happy in the knowledge that I was helping the ani-
mals I loved. It was not an easy goal. Earning the credentials, par-
ticularly the federal license that allows me to work with migratory
birds, took several years. I volunteered at wildlife shelters, studied
books, attended workshops and conferences, and collected cages and
medical supplies. I paid for everything myself, knowing that the work
I would use it for would be unpaid. I gathered letters of recommen-
dation and declarations of need from veterinarians, the National Park
Service, and the U.S. Coast Guard. Finally, in 1993, I received my
licenses.

By then, however, I knew that wildlife rehabilitation was not all
fun. In ideal circumstances rehabilitators only save, on the average,
half of their cases. On Ocracoke almost all of my patients are birds,
many of them water birds, among the most difficult animals to reha-
bilitate. Services are minimal, with only part-time veterinary assis-
tance on the island and no x-ray machine or lab facilities. I found
that my new calling meant dealing as much with death as with life.

Death has become a part of my daily existence. I see it not
only in my rehabilitation work. When I go to the ocean and soundside

beaches I find the remains of sea turtles, dolphins, or pelicans. When I walk along the road, I see tiny piles of feathers or smudges of fur; "road kill," they're called. Knowing my concern, people on the island contact me when there is a shearwater die-off, a dying cat, a dead whale stranding. I know that death is a natural part of life; the only part, in fact, upon which one can absolutely depend. Yet it never ceases to puzzle me, to sadden me. It is a shadow hovering constantly over me, tinting my brightest moods with a touch of darkness.

Its cream-colored belly was pressed tight against the black sulphurous earth. Its green and brown mottled skin, moist and cool, melted into the blades of bermuda grass which wove themselves into a protective tapestry around it. Overhead an emerald green, medallion-shaped pennywort leaf served as both parasol and shield, blocking out the drying rays of the sun and providing protection from the eyes of enemies. That yellow striped cat, the one that lived on the deck, had been lurking nearby earlier. This seemed like a safe spot, tucked away near the fence by the garden; a good place for a Fowlers toad, *Bufo woodhousei,* to spend the morning.

Not far away, I was trying out my newly sharpened and reconditioned lawn mower. It was the old-fashioned kind that does not have a motor; powered strictly by human muscle. Most of my yard was salt marsh, and the small area of higher land that I tried to maintain as a lawn could be cut with my ecological non-gasoline-burning mower. I hummed an old Rolling Stones tune to myself as I pushed it back and forth across the resistant grass.

"You're doing that the hard way, Pat," called Nathan, an old friend, as he drove by. "Builds muscles." I replied with a smile. Pushing steadily, I worked my way toward the fence that partitions off my vegetable garden. It felt good to be outside working on this crisp autumn day.

One moment I was happily forcing the metal blades through the thick tangle of grass; the next I was staring at the limp, twitching body of the Fowlers Toad. It took a few seconds to register what had happened. Where had the toad, one of my favorite of all creatures, come from? What had happened to it?

Slowly it dawned on me. I lifted it gently in my hand, hoping to see it shake its head in disgruntlement and hop off. But it lay still. I stared at the white line that sliced across its back, and I numbly wondered if toads pumped white blood in their tiny veins.

A strange thought crossed my mind. I was back in tenth grade biology class, and my teacher was irate with me because I refused to dissect the formaldehyde-soaked bullfrog that was provided for my learning pleasure. He called me into his office after class and bemoaned the fact that I could never be a wildlife biologist (as he knew I wanted) if I refused to dissect anything. "Then I won't be," I answered.

I managed to avoid participating in the Biol 101-102 dissection labs in college as well; but now, years later, I had finally dissected my frog. "Perhaps I should go get the carpetknife out of the toolbox and finish the job," I thought to myself. "Maybe now I can be a wildlife biologist;" but I was not really amused.

I carried the little amphibian into the flower garden and laid it under a shasta daisy plant. Its camouflage, the perfect defense against natural enemies, had proved its undoing this time. *Maybe it's just in shock; maybe the wound isn't as bad as it looks*, I thought without much hope.

I glumly went back to my grass-cutting, the pleasure gone now. Twice I checked on the toad. At first I couldn't find it, and my heart leapt as I thought it had awakened and hopped away. But no, there it was, and it hadn't moved. Finally, a few hours later, I took some of the garden soil and gently covered it. There was to be no vindication for me; the toad was dead and I had killed it.

I thought about death a lot that day. As I drove through the village I noticed several brown smudges on the road whose outlines revealed that they had once been happily hopping toads. They had no doubt been run over by drivers who had no idea that they had just snuffed out a life. Their moods had not been spoiled, their days not overcast by this shadow of guilt. I envied them. *If only I didn't know I'd killed it*, I thought wistfully. Hmm. Was that what I was really unhappy about? Not the actual death of the toad, but the suffering that my knowledge of its death brought me? Perhaps I wasn't as kind-hearted as I thought.

Why was I so upset about it anyway? That very morning I had squeezed ear mite medicine into my cats' ears, causing mass genocide, no doubt; wiping out entire villages of innocent mites as they went about their business. I had not felt sorry or guilty then. Who was to say that a toad's life had more value than that of an ear mite? Was I influenced by childhood memories of Thorton Burgess' *Grandfather Frog* and the obstreperous but lovable Mr. Toad in Kenneth Grahame's *Wind in the Willows*?

I wonder that same thing sometimes when I feed fish to injured water birds; mice to hawks; earthworms to robins. The question arises again when I sit down to a dinner of fried chicken, flounder, or crab cakes. Who determines that my life has more value than that of my dinner?

I often contemplate the pros and cons of becoming a vegetarian. Yet I consider myself to be a part of the natural world, and it is Mother Nature herself that has ordained the life and death, eat and be eaten cycle that makes it run. I doubt that she really cares whether we choose to be vegetarians or meat-eaters; wildlife rehabilitators or hunters; slayers of ear mites or mourners of slain toads. The moral questions we ask and the judgments we make are more for our own consolation, I suspect, than for some greater good.

As human beings, however, we ask the questions; and all the great religions try and help us find the answers. How, for example, do we compare the life of a toad to that of a person? It is certain that I, great animal lover as I am, would have been far more upset had the life I mowed down that morning been that of a human being. Surely humans value the life of their own kind above those of other species. Yet humans are almost the only animals that purposely set out to kill others of their own kind. I thought about the television movie I had turned on the night before, in which American soldiers in the Mexican War complained that they had not yet had a chance to shoot anyone. In the case of wars, human beings not only condone killing other humans; they celebrate it. How do we make sense of that?

Late that afternoon as I rode my bicycle home from the store, a bag of groceries balanced in my basket, I saw something move in front of me. There on the side of the road, waving its claws like a pint-sized hitch-hiker, was a blue crab. Sometimes I steer around fiddler and ghost crabs on the roads of Ocracoke, both species being land crabs. But this was a *Callinectes sapidus*; a "beautiful swimmer" which lives exclusively in the briny environs of estuaries and ocean. I looked around me. The ditch beside the road contained only an inch or so of water and had no outlet to the sound. There was no other water in sight.

"What on earth are you doing here?" I exclaimed, indulging my anthropomorphic weakness for conversing with animals.

It was not quite full grown, not a "keeper" as my family called the legal sized ones. Its claws had not yet developed the bright blue color that gives the crabs their common name, but were greenish brown, as was the rest of its body. It was not going to reach adulthood if it stayed here. If it didn't get hit by a car it would soon dehydrate in the hot sun.

Reaching gingerly behind it so that it could not seize my fingers, I picked it up by the shell and clambered back onto my bicycle "Bet you've never been for a bike ride before, huh?"

Apparently the crab was well versed, however, in crab bicycle riding etiquette. It stretched its legs and "swimmers" straight out and up, tucked its claws under its chin, and looked as if it was quite enjoying itself as it soared down the road, held high above the asphalt in my hand.

I turned down the sandy lane that leads to Pamlico Sound near my house. As we drew near the shore and it sensed the nearby presence of water, it abandoned its quiet stance and began wildly waving its legs and claws. I set it down in the sand and watched as it scurried into the water and disappeared into the vast, dark estuary. It might end up as a crab cake some day, but for now it was safe and alive.

As I stood there I thought, *I've taken a life today and I've saved one. Is that a fair trade? Would Mr. Toad forgive me now, if he was watching the exchange?* I wondered if I had evened the score or if, indeed, anyone was keeping score? If so, how did he/she determine and compare the value of a life? Was it based on size? Longevity? Intelligence? The price per pound of frog legs compared to backfin crabmeat?

Wondering about such things seems to be one of the defining attributes—perhaps even a requirement—of being human. Maybe it helps create and define our own personal rules for living. Perhaps it helps us learn to deal with our own inevitable dying. And maybe, just maybe, it will one day help us make this a better place to live, for humans and for animals alike. At any rate, I don't know that I've come any closer to solving the enigma of life and death. The only concrete result of all this soul-searching and ruminating is the surety that next time, before I cut my lawn, I'll shuffle my feet through the grass and make sure there's no one hiding there.

Seaweed for lunch

When I first arrived at Ocracoke, I was fascinated with the idea of living off the sea, and I set my crabpots and fish net accordingly. Having come of age in the time of Euell Gibbons' books on reaping the land and the sea, I hoped to harvest not only the fauna of the sound and ocean but the flora as well, which meant seaweed. Alas, I was to learn that few of Gibbon's seaweed recipes were based on plants of the mid-Atlantic seaboard. I gave it a try anyway but wasn't impressed.

Through the years, however, I remained intrigued with the plant life in the sea and sound and became amazed at how little most people, including myself, knew about it. Whole ecosystems—forests and meadows, jungles and floating gardens—sprout, grow, and die there to little notice from humans.

A stiff breeze kicked up whitecaps on Pamlico Sound. On a late morning walk, I scanned the shallow water lapping the shore and spied a translucent piece of green seaweed. It was attached to an oyster shell, both of which had been wrenched from the bottom by a storm the night before. The seaweed feathered out into attractive, delicate lime-colored leaves, but when I picked it out of the water it collapsed into a slimy glob of algae. I took a timid bite. Not surprisingly, it was sandy and salty, tasting of the sea. I gathered several more handfuls before calling Huck and heading for home. I had just found lunch.

Although I knew little about marine plant life, I had always wanted to learn more, and my interest had been spurred during my trip to Maritime Canada where I discovered a seaweed "fishery." Now I was determined to increase my knowledge.

According to Mark E. Hay and John P. Sutherland, 303 species of seaweed are found in North Carolina waters. Many grow near Ocracoke. Mark Fonseca, an ecologist at the NOAA laboratory in Morehead City, explains that what most people call seaweed are two distinct types of plants. The marine grasses are rooted and have runners much like land grasses. The true seaweeds, though, are all forms of algae.

Three kinds of sea grass grow in the estuaries near Ocracoke. Eel grass (*Zostera marina*) grows in deeper waters and has prominent flowers that bloom in winter. Widgeon grass (*Ruppie maritima*) grows almost anywhere, flowering profusely, while shoal grass (*Halodule wrightii*) prefers shallow waters and produces small inconspicuous flowers in summer.

Sometimes referred to as SAV (submerged aquatic vegetation), sea grass beds are among the most productive ecosystems on the planet, producing the equivalent of wheat and corn fields on land but without the requirement of fertilizers. They provide shelter for bay scallops, juvenile fish, and crabs; nourishment for migrating waterfowl, which feed on the roots, tubers, and seeds; and sustenance for invertebrates which feed on the decaying grass. They help anchor the sea floor and produce significant levels of oxygen, necessary for marine animal life. They also filter and trap sediments that can cloud the water and bury oysters and other bottom-dwelling organisms. They remove pollutants such as nitrogen and phosphorus, which enter the water from sewage systems, farms and urban lawns and in excess cause harmful algal blooms. As an example of the importance of sea grass beds, scientists say that 30 times more juvenile crabs live in grass beds than in comparable areas without them. North Carolina has some 200,000 acres of sea grass beds.

Eel grass, which washes up on the shores of Pamlico Sound, makes an excellent garden fertilizer. I carry numerous bagsful home from the beach near my house each year and spread it on my gardens. Mark Fonseca told me how the Cabot Quilt Company once sewed eel grass into paper liners which were used to insulate buildings. The salt and silica in the grass served as a flame retardant. In former days at Ocracoke eel grass was used to line pig pens, making soft dry beds for the animals.

The true seaweeds include both rooted, or benthic, and unrooted, or pelagic, algae. Many of the pelagic varieties are microscopic dynoflagellates. Micro-algae, the blue-green slime often seen growing in creeks and canals, are one of the most important plants in the estuary, an easy-to-digest source of food for invertebrates and post-larval fishes. They have lived on earth for two billion years and are believed by some scientists to have been the source of the earth's first atmospheric oxygen. They can be pelagic or benthic.

Benthic algae attach themselves to a hard surface using a structure known as a holdfast, which leads along a stipe to the leaf-like blades. The entire plant is known as a thallus. Some are annuals, some perennials. Many are seasonal, growing in either warm or cold months, then becoming dormant or dying. They reproduce by sexual and asexual means, some by both.

Red algae species are more numerous than green and brown seaweeds. They require less light so they can grow at greater depths. *Porphvra*, or purple dye seaweed, is a paper-thin, transparent species which is edible. Another species living in Ocracoke waters, *Gracilaria*, or sewing thread seaweed, is a source of agar, which is used to make hand lotions, shoe polish, cosmetics, and in photo developing processes. This bushy alga, which grows to a foot or more in height, has reddish brown to olive green spaghetti-like branches.

The brown algae living near Ocracoke include rockweeds and sargassum, or gulfweed. Large seaweeds, they have air pockets, or bladders, which help them float close to the surface and absorb sunlight. Several species of sargassum weed live in the warm waters of the Gulf Stream off the Carolina coast. Some are attached, others pelagic, floating here from the Sargasso Sea. They grow from five to 30 miles off Ocracoke and support an amazing array of sea life, including sea horses, baby loggerhead turtles, dolphin fish, marlin and tuna.

As I read the newspaper one morning, I was surprised to see a headline announcing a ban on seaweed harvesting in North Carolina. I didn't know anyone harvested it. Reading further, I learned about a small business in Beaufort that had been collecting sargassum weed and selling it as a supplement for livestock feed and organic fertilizer for more than 20 years. Because of the plant's importance to the marine ecosystem, however, the South Atlantic Fishery Management Council decided the ban was justified.

All of this knowledge was to come after I found the seaweed that was to become my lunch. This was sea lettuce (*ulva lactuca*), a kind of green algae. Because green algae need plentiful light, they grow in shallow estuarine waters like the tidal flat where I found mine. In earlier readings, I had found various ways to use sea lettuce. It could be pressed into a chewing plug as a substitute for tobacco (I decided to pass on that one). It also could be ground for seasoning, or put into salads and sandwiches. I planned to have a seaweed sandwich.

Back in my kitchen, I pulled the sea lettuce loose from the shells to which it clung, washed the grit and eel grass out of the leaves, and sprinkled it with salt, pepper and lemon. I slathered two slices of whole wheat bread with mayonnaise and spicy brown mustard, piled them high with sea lettuce and took a bite. Not bad. Not bad at all.

I put the remainder of my sea lettuce in the oven to dry, planning to crumble it later and use it as an herb. Maybe making "seaweed spices" will be my next enterprise. Or perhaps I'll open a trendy new restaurant called Seaweed by the Sea. If you see me driving a new Mercedes instead of an old pickup, you'll know that seaweed was my soggy ticket to success.

Kemps Ridley sea turtles: our ocean in distress

When I first moved to Ocracoke in 1984 it seemed to be an island out of time, protected from the twentieth century and its vagaries by the waters that surround it. Gradually, time has been catching up with it. Businesses and summer rental cottages are springing up in almost every buildable space. Land Use Plans, intended to preserve the environmental and cultural uniqueness of the island, have come and gone, with only limited success. Fortunately for those of us who love the old Ocracoke, most of it is protected by its status as a National Seashore. As long as that stays in place we will be spared the worst of the developers and money-mongers. We still have no traffic lights or chain stores, no shopping malls or golf courses. People still pause to chat at the Post Office while collecting their daily mail; and drivers still stop and visit in the roads when they meet, as those behind them wait good-naturedly or go around.

But the inexorable, unrelenting wheel of "progress" grinds on, and none of us who loved Ocracoke the way it was has been able to stop it. Even my little corner of the island at Marsh Haven is susceptible. Lots are being sold and houses built within hollering distance. I recently learned that the salt marsh near my house, supposedly protected as a coastal wetland, may have a bridge built across it. Some day soon automobiles may lumber where once marsh hawks soared.

What tomorrow holds will depend on whether those who live here choose to preserve the island or to exploit it. But Ocracoke is no longer a world unto itself. Its future depends also upon the well-being of the global environment, particularly of the ocean and sound that encradle it.

The coffee pot was on, the cats happily munching on their breakfast, and Huck and I had come down to the beach for our morning walk. (I was walking, that is. Huck was hurtling through the shallows of Pamlico Sound, chasing a couple of herring gulls who were not, I'm sure, the least bit frightened but no doubt annoyed, possibly even amused, as they watched his silly antics from 10 feet above.) It was another idyllic day, temperatures in the 70s, cloudless sky overhead. We had been enjoying beautiful balmy May weather these past few weeks. The odd thing was, it was not May but December.

I was taking advantage of this unusual opportunity to go barefooted and jacketless, though I rather missed the biting tang that late fall usually brings. I wandered down the beach, observing otter tracks leading back to the canal and large heron tracks near the water (maybe a great blue). I noticed how high the eel grass was piled up today and remarked to myself that I should come down and get a bag for my garden.

My pleasure turned to sadness when I saw, nestled in a pile of that eel grass, the carcass of a turtle. The carapace was tannish gray and heart-shaped, about 12 inches long. It was a Kemps Ridley, the smallest and most endangered of the world's sea turtles. My discovery put a damper on my morning expedition. I mulled over it later that day as I balanced on a wooden scaffold, painting window trim on a house. Was the turtle death an isolated incident, or did it indicate some new crisis in the ocean or estuaries?

I mentioned finding the turtle to Marcia Lyons, the National Park Service naturalist, and she told me that an unprecedented number of Kemps Ridley strandings had taken place in the past few weeks on and around Ocracoke. She suggested that I call Ruth Boettcher, of the N.C. Wildlife Resources Commission, to report my find. I did, and the next day Ruth came by my house to pick it up for examination.

The Kemps Ridley (*Lepidochelys kempi*) is one of seven major species of sea turtles that live in the oceans of the world. All but one are protected under the Endangered Species Act and five occur, at least occasionally, in the waters off Ocracoke Island. Loggerheads are seen most frequently; it is rare to see a Kemps Ridley. It was doubly disturbing, therefore, to find one dead.

Ridleys can weigh up to 100 pounds and are almost as wide as they are long. They feed primarily on crabs, but also eat mollusks and other invertebrates, as well as some seaweeds. For many years no one knew where Kemps Ridleys bred or nested. In fact, according to naturalist Jack Rudloe, they were sometimes called "bastard turtles" since their origins were unknown. The mystery was solved when, in

1961, an amateur film from Mexico was discovered. It showed a 1947 arribada, or "emergence;" an amazing display of 40,000 female Kemps Ridleys laying eggs on one long beach.

Now scientists know that Kemps Ridleys nest primarily at one beach near Rancho Nuevo in the western Gulf of Mexico. They come ashore some windy day between April and July and lay an average of 100 eggs each. The hatchlings appear after 45-58 days. Juvenile ridleys move up and down the eastern seaboard of the United States, migrating with the seasons. The one which I found would have been making its way south to the Gulf of Mexico for the winter.

The population of these small sea turtles has declined dramatically in the last 50 years. The number of nesting females for one day went from 40,000 in 1947, as seen on the filmstrip, to an average of only 200 during the years of 1978 to 1991. Biologists worry that they are on the brink of extinction.

According to Ruth, there were 67 Kemps Ridley strandings documented in North Carolina in 1998, the largest number reported in the state in a single year. Most (41) took place in the three-month period between October 1 and December 31. The majority of these were found between Shackleford Banks and Hatteras Island, with Ocracoke having the highest incidence. Most (including the one I found) were on the sound rather than the ocean side.

These were the facts Ruth gave me. The unanswered questions were far more numerous. Little is known about the life history of this marine reptile, which turtle expert Dr. Archie Carr called "the most mysterious animal in North America." To many of the questions I asked Ruth, she replied, "Nobody knows." This was the answer she gave when I asked what was killing the ridleys washing up at Ocracoke.

Could their deaths, I wondered, be the result of the abnormally warm temperatures we were enjoying? I knew that unusual environmental conditions could affect animal behavior patterns, leading to adverse results. Local fishermen and duck hunters had their own ideas. They told me about unprecedented numbers of dead ridley, loggerhead, and green sea turtles that they had seen this fall, and they blamed it on expansion of deep water gill netting in Pamlico Sound. Whatever the cause, chances were good that their deaths were the result of human actions.

The stranding incidence of the Kemps Ridley sea turtles was the issue of main concern on Ocracoke that week, but the plight of our oceans and estuaries is far broader and more inclusive. Sea turtle strandings are nothing new at Ocracoke. Dead loggerheads wash up on the beach frequently, some killed in trawl nets, some hit by boats, most dead from unknown causes. Dying loons come ashore with high levels of mercury; cormorants show elevated concentrations of both mercury and selenium. Tests on sick dolphins reveal toxic levels of TBT (tributyltin), a notorious paint additive used in large shipyards.

A recent, first-of-its-kind study of the Atlantic Ocean and Gulf of Mexico, done at Harvard University, concluded that the oceans are in trouble and so are we. Whale, dolphin, and porpoise strandings increased from nearly zero in 1972 to almost 1,400 in 1994. Mass fish kills and disease outbreaks increased more than a hundredfold in the last 20 years. Human health problems caused by contact with the ocean increased from two reported incidents in 1966 to 118 in 1996. Harmful algae blooms, sometimes called Red Tides, were more than four times as common in 1996 as in 1976.

The main villains, they concluded, are nutrient pollution and increasing water temperatures. The two go hand in hand. Nutrient pollution is caused by the release into our waters of fertilizers and effluent from sewage systems and animal farms. It causes algae blooms which deplete the water of oxygen, and provide an ideal environment for the proliferation of dangerous phytoplankton, such as pfiesteria. Elevated water temperatures from global warming can make algal blooms even worse.

Global warming and climate change, once considered a controversial issue espoused by radical environmentalists, is now regarded by most scientists as fact. While there is no definitive proof of what is causing it, plenty of facts verify its existence. According to an Associated Press report from Toronto, Canada, "there is nothing hypothetical about climate change in the far north." Ice fields are already melting, and Canada's sub-Arctic regions could face widespread chaos.

The World Meteorological Organization reports that 1998 was the warmest year on record, and that temperatures had been rising steadily for 10 years. While some of the warming is attributed to natural causes, most scientists agree that at least part of the temperature increase is due to human causes, particularly what are called "greenhouse gases," such as carbon dioxide from factory and automobile emissions.

What do these issues mean for Ocracoke? Rising sea levels from glacial melting in the north is one concern. Is it coincidence that my neighbor Danny Wynne says he has never, in the 21 years he has lived here, seen flooding like we've had this year (and we did not even have a major hurricane)? Tangier Island, in the Chesapeake Bay, is disappearing as its residents watch; being submerged as water levels rise, due in part to glacial melting. If global warming continues as predicted Marsh Haven could one day be a haven for bluefish and flounder.

Walking along the beach, one might see the remnants of a bottle-nose dolphin, a northern gannet, a loggerhead sea turtle, or maybe a pilot whale or a harbor seal. Most will have died as a result of some human-related cause. A brown pelican I presently have in my care may, according to a wildlife veterinarian I consulted, be suffering from the results of ingesting fish contaminated with harmful algae. It is believed that these algae are proliferating due to the unusually warm water temperatures.

Climate change, brought about by global warming, causes unusual, often violent, weather conditions. One evening in early September a waterspout, spawned in the wake of Hurricane Danielle, lifted a house at Ocracoke off its foundation, carried it high into the air, and dropped it into the sea. The next morning Ocracokers flocked to the spot where the house had formerly stood, staring in wonder. There was nothing to see, just a foundation with a few boards and household items scattered about.

"Never saw the like of that before," marveled one oldtimer. "The weather's been doing strange things." Staring at the empty foundation, another Ocracoke resident shook his head. "There you go," he said. "You don't mess with Mother Nature!"

We humans have messed with Mother Nature, whether by unwise exploitation of our natural resources or by the creation of products whose long-term effects we do not understand. There is a price to pay, and the dolphins and whales, the loons and Kemps Ridley sea turtles are already paying it. So will the rest of us, if we do not reverse the direction in which we are headed.

I'll be glad when the young Kemps Ridley sea turtles, now on their journey south, get past Pamlico Sound and whatever is causing their deaths here. And even though I'm enjoying these spring-like days (which may, after all, be a fluke weather system unrelated to climate change,) I'll be relieved when winter arrives in earnest. I may gripe about freezing fingertips and frozen pipes, but I'd rather put up with Mother Nature's sometimes harsh rules than with the ecological anarchy that too much human interference may bring about.

Sauntering at Ocracoke

After spending two weeks in Richmond while my mother underwent an unexpected surgery, I was ensconced again in my old routine at Ocracoke, which actually meant no routine. Writing, painting, making sea glass jewelry, working a few hours at Island Artworks, selling a bit of yaupon tea, kayaking out to an island to rescue a pelican wrapped in fishing line; I never knew what each day would bring. What I did know was that I had some things to puzzle out about myself.

While traveling in Newfoundland and Labrador I had found something I had thought was lost: myself. My old self, that is; the person who had wandered to Ocracoke 14 years before from the Caribbean with not a dollar or a worry to her name. She was carefree and happy-go-lucky, unencumbered with the concerns that I now had, untouched by the despair that sometimes settled over me like a dark cloud. I liked her, and I wasn't sure I wanted to let her go again.

On the other hand, sometimes I thought about having a normal life with a "real" job; one with a set schedule and a regular paycheck. I wondered what it would be like to drive a new car, go to a restaurant and a movie every week, maybe even work on my Ph.D. I even imagined having a home where August and September did not mean "hurricane season."

Yet I loved my life at Ocracoke. I loved my little house and all the work I was forever having to do to it. I loved working with the animals, both wild and tame. I loved my patchwork style of earning a living, and the independent, strong-minded people who resided here. Most of all, I loved the close connection with nature that being on the island made not only possible, but requisite. I wasn't sure what I wanted to do in the future, what path I would choose to follow (or if, indeed, I would have a choice). For now, I was glad to be at Ocracoke again, doing exactly what I was doing.

I had just met the deadline, though barely, for a story I had contracted to write for the *Island Breeze*. It was too late to mail it, so I called Huck and we hopped in my truck and drove up to the ferry station at the north end of the island. I handed it to the captain. "Would you please deliver this to the Hatteras Ferry Station? Someone will pick it up there." Knowing it was in safe hands, I walked back to my truck and breathed a sigh of relief.

My story was on its way, and I had nothing pressing for the rest of this gorgeous autumn afternoon. I still had my kayak tied to the top of my camper shell. I looked in the back of the truck and exclaimed with joy when I saw that the paddles were there too.

"How'd you like to go kayaking, Huck?" I asked. He tilted his head to the side, one ear up, and looked at me with that pleading expression I knew meant "Yes Mom. Please, please, please."

I had never kayaked this far up the island, so I drove slowly, searching for a road we could take to the sound. After a mile or so I found a sandy lane, bordered by wax myrtle and cedar trees. I put my truck into four-wheel-drive and headed down it. Winding around curves, up a few hillocks, and down into a few precarious-looking ditches filled with water, we finally came to the shore of Pamlico Sound.

Huck frolicked in the shallow water, sniffing through the piles of eel grass for washed up crabs and other items of interest, while I untied the kayak and slid it off the camper shell. It was quiet here, the only vestige of human life a stake blind out on the reef. Since it was not yet hunting season I guessed that it was unoccupied.

Dragging the kayak into the water, I waded in, sat down, and called Huck. He came running and dove into the front amid a splattering of cold water and mud. "Thanks, boy," I chided him as I wiped a splotch of mud off my cheek. He settled into his favorite kayaking position, sitting upright between my knees, and we set off, heading north.

The shoreline seemed to stretch forever, a solid, unending curtain of marsh grass; but before long I came to an opening. I was delighted to see that a creek wended its way into the marsh, cutting a path that seemed to invite me and my kayak to follow. It soon opened into a labyrinth of meandering waterways, each lined with softly rustling spartina grass and ribbed mussels. I paddled my way slowly along them.

I'd take a few strokes to guide us in a general direction or push us off the marshgrass, then we'd drift a little. We watched diamondback terrapins slide off the banks and pop their heads up out of the water, enjoying these last warm days before digging into the mud for winter. We listened as kingfishers scolded us with loud staccato voices when we accidentally rousted them from their cedar branch perches. We spotted a rookery of 15 great blue herons clinging to the branches of a low hummock and swooping, terradactyl-like, over the water in search of a meal. I leaned back and gazed at the distant silhouette of a squadron of brown pelicans as they soared low above the water, bridging the horizon between sky and sound.

As I paddled idly along I thought of a chapter I had recently read in Anne La Bastille's *Beyond Black Bear Lake*, an autobiographical account of a woman living in the Adirondack mountains. In the chapter entitled "Sauntering Around Lilypad Lake" she told how she "sauntered" slowly and without direction around the pond where she had built her cabin. She explained that as she sauntered she was "free, unobtainable, detached...and open to adventure." She had borrowed the word, she said, from Henry David Thoreau, the nineteenth century naturalist after whose cabin at Walden Pond she had patterned her own.

Upon reading her chapter I had gone to the library and checked out a collection of Thoreau's work. I found his description of the word saunter in the essay "Walking." According to Thoreau, "sauntering" is a fourth estate, outside of Church and State and People. It must be without direction or specific purpose, but it is never a form of idleness. He says that "we should go forth on the shortest walk, perchance, in the spirit of undying adventure, never to return...if you have paid your debts, and made your will, and settled all your affairs, and are a free man, then you are ready for a walk....Moreover, you must walk like a camel, which is said to be the only beast which ruminates when walking."

I found three possible origins for the word "saunter." Webster's *New World Dictionary* says that it comes from the Latin word *santren*, which means "to muse" (ponder or meditate). According to another explanation, it is derived from the French sans terre, "without land or home." Thoreau believed that it originated in the Middle Ages, when idle people roving about the country claimed to be going "a la Sainte Terre" (to the holy land) and were called "Sainte-Terrers" or Holy-Landers. To him sauntering was indeed a kind of search for a holy land.

I was, I decided, as I paddled slowly along the creeks, sauntering myself; sauntering in a kayak instead of on foot. I have my own personal definition for the word. Sauntering is what people come to Ocracoke to do. It is slowing down, allowing not only the feet but the mind as well to wander where they will; to turn down new paths with no specific destinations in mind. It is a way of opening the soils of our minds so that new thoughts, new ideas, new dreams can take seed and flower; not the ones we deliberately plant, but those that may float in on a wisp of seafoam or a moonbeam.

Ocracoke is a great place for sauntering. Some visitors complain that there is nothing to do here; but it is that very fact that draws others back year after year. Without the frantic distractions of shopping malls, miniature golf courses, and video arcades people are forced to look within; to tread softly; to contemplate nature; to muse. I keep a journal available for those who rent my house each summer to record their thoughts. They often write about how stressed they are when they first arrive, but how the island soothes them. They gradually slow down, unwind, and discover peaceful oases within themselves. By the end of the week they have learned, or re-learned, to saunter. I wonder how long it takes them to forget again after they leave.

Many of us who live here have, I think, forgotten. There is a riddle on the island that goes something like this: "How do you tell a tourist from a local? The tourist has a suntan." There is a lot of truth to it; most residents work so hard during the "season" that they have neither time nor energy to spend outdoors. A friend of mine, a successful Ocracoke businessman, recently told me that he has to leave the island during the winter in order to relax. Why are we able to saunter on our vacations but not in our regular lives?

Perhaps it is because of guilt. Many of us are taught that sauntering through life is wrong; it does not fit our puritanical work ethic. We have it drilled into us at an early age that we should stay busy, do something all the time. We should always be "accomplishing something." Perhaps too it has something to do with the way we measure success. Many of us feel that we have somehow failed unless we have a new house, a fancy car, a wide-screened television, and an upscale computer. Thoreau felt that he was a failure if he did not have at least four hours a day to contemplate nature and life. The two views are not often compatible.

I was lucky. Somewhere in her teaching career my mother came across the term "spinning out." Children need time, she said, to just do nothing, to allow their minds to spin out to wherever they will. This, I think, is another form of sauntering. I was encouraged by my parents to spin out or to saunter, if you will, from an early age; and I have become quite an expert at it. I know how to saunter on the ocean beach, in the quiet back lanes of the village, even in my porch swing. For me it has become a necessity of life. For many, however, it is a luxury, an indulgence to be enjoyed only after it has been earned by hard work.

It is a mistake to confuse Thoreau's and La Bastille's concept of "sauntering" with laziness or idleness. Here on Ocracoke the term "Ocracoma" has evolved to describe a state of unmotivated, directionless, often alcohol-related sluggishness that the island's easy lifestyle can induce. This sluggishness can lead to a shutting down of the mind and soul; a form of mental inertia. Sauntering, on the contrary, implies an opening up...a liberation of one's innermost self so that it can reach for new horizons and learn from the natural world around it.

It is not practical, of course, to saunter all the time.

Sometimes I forget about the practical side of life and get carried away with the wandering and pondering. Then some pending deadline or overdue bill snatches me back to reality. Sometimes, too, I get caught up in the "rat race" and even find myself enjoying it. Having a busy schedule with no time for introspection or soul-searching can be a relief. Contrary to what many may think, I believe that hard work with long hours is a form of escapism; for if one stays busy enough he is spared the contemplation of the serious, often painful issues of life. Yet without this contemplation one misses much of life's beauty and meaning.

Walking for exercise, walking to reach a destination, working to obtain a goal; all are necessary and important components of life. But we often get so caught up in our goal-oriented lives that we become trapped on a treadmill and can't get off. How wonderful it is when we can achieve a balance between "sauntering" and "doing."

Finally I decided, with some reluctance, that it was time to head home. Once I made the decision and set my course, it took only a few minutes to cover the route where I had sauntered for hours. After loading the kayak on the truck I was soon on my way back. I had nothing concrete to show for my time, but I returned with the sensation of an afternoon well spent. Tomorrow I would concentrate on the necessity of earning a living; today I was happy to contemplate the pleasures and peculiarities of living itself.

Conclusion

My time at Ocracoke, it seems to me, has been a journey, not of place but of spirit. It has been a quest for a simpler way of living; a search for fulfillment not through material wealth, power, or status, but through rapport with the natural world and ultimately with my innermost self. It has to do with finding joy in the ordinary, magic in the mundane, and learning to live in harmony with the world around us.

Through it all there has been a feeling of rightness, of being where I belong, which brings me peace. Yet it has not always been an easy passage. Loneliness, the specter of death and suffering, and a constant struggle to make ends meet have honed the years into sharp, quickened blades that cut through the layers of daily existence, exposing both the agony and the ecstasy of life. It has been an odyssey in which great adventures, fearful adversaries, disheartening defeats, and thrilling accomplishments all play a part. The stories I relate in *Ocracoke Wild* and *Ocracoke Odyssey* are my accounts of this passage.

My experience has been an amazing journey but not a unique one. We are each embarked on a similar odyssey, trying to overcome our own demons, to resist our own sirens of temptation, and to chart a course that will lead us through smooth seas to some ephemeral shore we call happiness. It is my belief that unless we set a course that steers us in harmony with one another and the natural world, we will never reach that shore.